PELICAN BOOK A649

Studies in Social Pathology

EDITED BY G. M. CARSTAIRS

SEXUAL DEVIATION

ANTHONY STORR

Anthony Storr was born in 1920 and educated at
Winchester College and Christ's College,
Cambridge, where he studied medicine. After
qualifying as a doctor in 1944 he specialized in
psychiatry and held posts at Runwell Mental
Hospital and at the Maudsley Hospital. He also
trained as an analyst in the school of C. G. Jung,
though he prefers not to be labelled as an
adherent of any one analytical school. He has
contributed reviews and articles to many papers,
including the *New Statesman*, the *Observer*, the
Sunday Times, and *New Society*, and an earlier
book, *The Integrity of the Personality*, has already
appeared as a Pelican. Anthony Storr is married
and has three daughters.

Anthony Storr

Sexual Deviation

 Penguin Books

Penguin Books Ltd, Harmondsworth, Middlesex, England
Penguin Books Inc., 3300 Clipper Mill Road, Baltimore 11, Md, U.S.A.
Penguin Books Pty Ltd, Ringwood, Victoria, Australia

First published 1964
Reprinted 1964

Copyright © Anthony Storr, 1964

Made and printed in Great Britain by C. Nicholls & Company Ltd
Set in Monotype Times

Contents

Editorial Foreword

This book is the first of a new series of Pelicans which will discuss a number of important problems of contemporary life, under the general heading: Studies in Social Pathology. It will be followed by a succession of short monographs whose authors have shown themselves to be not only authorities in their respective fields, but also capable of discussing them in straightforward non-technical language. Among the subjects to be dealt with are: alcoholism, depression and suicide, the violent criminal, and the meaning of madness.

These are, quite literally, morbid subjects, examples of deviations of human behaviour which still have to be reckoned with in contemporary society; but the Pelicans in this series will not, I believe, pander to morbid curiosity. Their authors will be concerned to show how these things come about, and in so doing they will make it easier for us to look levelly at the deviants in our midst, deploring their actions but not totally rejecting the individuals themselves. As the title of the series implies all these are conditions in whose aetiology social factors play a major part. There, but for the grace of God, go we.

It may be surprising to some readers that sexual deviation should be included under this head. There has been a strong tendency in the past to regard all 'perverts' as the outcasts of humanity, a separate and despicable race of mankind deserving the severest forms of punishment. Dr Storr makes it plain that this view is quite erroneous. He maintains that sexual deviations can only be understood as failures in the quite complicated process of learning how to love; and he shows that every one of us has experienced in our own childhood or in the effective disguise of fashions and conventions which are so familiar that we have ceased to be aware of their significance, some of the feelings which take the place of normal sexual fulfilment for some of our fellow men and women.

No one would deny that sex is one of the major instinctual drives, and yet it differs from our other basic drives such as hunger, thirst, and breathing in that its physical realization is delayed until early adult life and associated with particularly complex patterns of social behaviour. Denial of air or food or water has fatal consequences; the consequences of failure to achieve sexual satisfaction are less obvious. People do not die as a result of sexual deprivation; but it seems probable that they may never live life to the full.

Dr Storr begins with a brief account of normal love relationships, and shows that these are most likely to be experienced by people who enjoyed a secure and affectionate family life in their infancy. The capacity to love another human being, he points out, depends in the first instance in having oneself been loved. In this mutual encounter of the sexes, each partner knows that he or she is loved in return. Individuals whose earliest infantile relationships were insecure find it hard to perceive themselves as lovable. For them, the challenge of physical love between man and woman becomes frightening and unattainable; they turn to substitutes in phantasy instead. In so doing, sexual deviants allay their neurotic fears, and may even achieve a certain happiness; but their failure to experience mature heterosexual relations limits that full self-realization which Dr Storr terms individuation.

Sexual deviants have taken a side turning, a blind alley, in the course of their progress towards sexual maturity. Dr Storr shows us how this comes about, how some of the deviants can be helped while a few may need to be restrained. In his account there is no room for condemnation but only for compassion towards these unfortunates in their predicament.

G. M. CARSTAIRS

1   Introduction

This book is an attempt to discuss some of the commoner sexual deviations, to give tentative explanations of their meanings, and to relate them to normal behaviour.

In Western society today we are only just beginning to study sexuality objectively, despite the fact that the sexual impulse is a basic and integral part of human nature which deeply affects the character and conduct of each one of us. The way in which an individual has or has not come to terms with his sexual instinct determines many aspects of his character, including both his confidence in himself and also his capacity for making relationships with other human beings. It is therefore important that we should know as much as possible about every aspect of our sexual nature, including those aspects which are generally labelled perverse or deviant.

This statement may be disputed; since many people would like to dissociate their erotic behaviour from the rest of their life and, in attempting to do so, treat sex as a fundamentally unimportant part of their existence. This is especially true of those who either have sexual difficulties which they are ashamed to acknowledge, or a secret sexual life which they feel bound to conceal. Such people find it a relief to pretend that sex can be relegated to a separate compartment of their lives, stored away in a safe deposit to which no other person is ever allowed access. But the front which people of this kind are compelled to present to the world is a dull, unemotional façade; for sex is so important, so pervasive, and so intimately connected with every aspect of personality that it cannot be separated from the person as a whole without impoverishing even superficial relationships. There are times when we meet other human beings simply to exchange information, or to discuss ideas, or in some professional setting. On such occasions the sexual aspect of ourselves is of minimal importance. But directly we meet people socially as people, our attitude to our own sexuality and to theirs becomes significant; for the kind of contact which we make with each other in ordinary social exchanges at a superficial level is determined by the capacity we possess for making deeply intimate relationships; and the ideal sexual relationship is probably the deepest and most intimate which we can experience.

The very words we use express the fact that, fundamentally, it is impossible to separate physical from mental in inter-personal relations. For do we not talk of *making contact* with another; of a person's *warmth* or *coldness*; of being *close* to someone or *distant*; and of being *touched* by another's interest or thoughtfulness? We are not, and cannot be, disembodied; and so our attitude to our own bodies and to those of other people is an important part of our total feeling towards even those with whom we may never exchange any more intimate gesture than a handshake. It is because of this that those who are ill-at-ease with their own sexuality are often detached and remote; for they are unable to allow their sexual selves to be manifest, and thus withdraw, both physically and psychologically, from the possibility of close contact. On the other hand, those who have been able to find sexual happiness are not generally afraid of intimacy, and are thus less guarded and more able to interchange experience at even purely social levels of relationship.

Since sex is so important a part of the human condition, it might be supposed that the scientifically minded nations of the West would long ago have discerned and codified all that could possibly be discovered about it. Yet it is only in recent years that we have sufficiently discarded prejudice for science to begin the objective investigation of the actual sexual behaviour of men and women. There has never been any shortage of authorities who are prepared to tell us what our sexual behaviour ought to be;

but there has been a notable lack of information as to what it actually is. Kinsey and his associates have done much to remedy our ignorance; and no writer on sex can fail to acknowledge the debt which he must owe to their research. But there are still many aspects of sexuality upon which we are ill-informed, and this is especially so in the case of the so-called sexual deviations.

The use of the term deviation implies the existence of a standard of normality from which deviation may take place; but no absolute standard can be found, for what is considered to be sexually normal varies widely both from country to country and from epoch to epoch. A sexual practice which is considered acceptable in one time and place may be abhorred as a perversion in another; and even within the same culture, each individual may adhere to a different standard of sexual behaviour, depending upon the interaction between his upbringing and the strength of his sexual needs. It is safe to assert that there is no sexual practice which has not somewhere been condemned, and none which has not elsewhere been accepted. Incest, for example, was enjoined upon the Pharaohs, though generally regarded as undesirable for lesser mortals. What constitutes incest is, however, variously defined; and, in some cultures, any form of cross-cousin marriage is forbidden. In certain states of the U.S.A., mouth-genital contacts, both fellatio and cunnilinctus, which are widely recognized elsewhere as part of normal love-making, are legally regarded as 'crimes against nature', and can be the subject of savage penalties; whilst some religious codes have even alleged that all positions in marital coitus save one are to be condemned. In this country we have only recently emerged from an era in which masturbation was not only regarded as unnatural, but actually held responsible for mental illness; and, even now, some adolescents suffer torments of conscience on this account, although masturbation is so universal a practice that ninety-three per cent of males and sixty-two per cent of females have some experience of it. Sado-masochism, the name given to the deviation in which erotic excitement is experienced in connexion with the infliction or reception of pain, is commonly regarded as perverse. Yet, judging by the popularity of books and films in which sexually-tinged violence plays a part, sado-masochistic phantasies must be practically universal, although there are many who recoil from the admission that such thoughts have ever played a part in their own erotic imaginings.

Since what is sexually deviant and what normal cannot accurately be determined, it might be thought that to write upon sexual deviation is an impossible task. Nevertheless, it is probable that the readers to whom this book is addressed would agree in broad outline as to what is considered sexually abnormal in our own society. We should all, for instance, concur in regarding a man whose sexual desire is directed exclusively towards small children as abnormal (a view which would almost certainly be shared by the man himself); and we should probably all agree that the exhibitionistic exposure of the genitals is a deviant way of obtaining sexual gratification. But there would certainly be disagreement upon homosexuality, since there are some who vehemently condemn homosexual behaviour, whilst others look upon it as perfectly normal.

Although it may be impossible to define normality in sexual behaviour even within the confines of a single society, there do exist other standards in terms of which it is possible to make comparative appraisals. One such standard is that of emotional maturity, a concept which is found under various guises in the writings of every psychodynamic school. It is a standard to which no human being ever attains and is therefore an ideal at which to aim rather than an actual achievement. But, although the emphasis varies from writer to writer, there is so much agreement upon what constitutes maturity that the concept provides a useful yardstick against which to measure deviation, whether this be in the sexual or in some other field of human behaviour.

As displayed in the sexual sphere, maturity may be defined as the ability to form a stable relationship with the opposite sex which is both physically and emotionally satisfying, and in which sexual intercourse forms the main, though not the only, mode of expression of love. It is those whose emotional development is retarded so that they cannot reach maturity who show deviations from this standard. These deviations take various forms. In some instances a person of the same sex or a child is sought as a sexual companion. In others, although the partner may be both adult and of the opposite sex, intercourse is avoided and some other act substituted for it. In still others, no second person is directly involved, but sexual gratification is obtained from objects other than people, or from observing the sexual activities of others. These various substitutes for intercourse will be discussed in subsequent chapters.

It is assumed that, for the mature person, heterosexual intercourse is generally the most rewarding way of obtaining sexual satisfaction, and that it will therefore be the chief sexual aim for most people most of the time. This is not to say that it is the only aim, or that normal people never substitute other sexual practices for intercourse, or make use of fetishistic or sado-masochistic rituals as preliminaries to sexual union. They very commonly do so. We all carry within us the seeds of every sexual deviation. But the truly deviant person habitually turns away from, or is unable to achieve heterosexual intercourse; and so one or other of the sexual interests which form a subsidiary part of the average person's erotic life becomes, for him, the essential or only possible way of obtaining sexual release. It is the compulsive substitution of something else for heterosexual intercourse in circumstances where the latter is available which chiefly characterizes the behaviour we call sexually deviant.

Psychoanalytic writers have often been criticized for equating sexual maturity with emotional maturity. It has been pointed out, for instance, that many homosexuals are stable, balanced people whom everyone would regard as mature except in their sexual tastes; and it is obvious that there are people in whom heterosexuality is well established, but who behave in other ways as if they had never left the nursery. Nevertheless, it is still true to say that heterosexuality is a more mature form of sexual behaviour than homosexuality; and, although the correlation between emotional maturity and sexual maturity is far from perfect, we can assert with some confidence that, ideally, the mature person is one who is not only heterosexual, but whose sexual behaviour is consistent with the rest of his behaviour, and thus not treated by him or by others as separate from his personality as a whole.

When we begin to discuss personality as a whole, we are immediately involved in discussing relationships between persons. For no one can be said to exist as a person if he is unrelated to other persons. A person requires relationships with other persons for his own definition; and if we call a man strong or weak, good or bad, tall or short, we are necessarily comparing him with another person, even if the latter be but a figure of phantasy. In discussing sex and sexual deviations, therefore, we are bound to be discussing various types of relationships between persons, for, although some sexual activities are carried on in solitude, the day dreams which accompany such activities usually include other persons or substitutes for persons; or if centred on the subject only, portray him in different roles. Solitary sexual activity is ultimately unsatisfying just because it is solitary.

Sexual intercourse may be said to be one aspect, perhaps the most basic and most important aspect, of a relationship between persons. In ideally mature form it is a relationship between a man and a woman in which giving and taking is equal, and in which the genitals are the most important channel through which love is expressed and received. It is one of the most natural, and certainly the most rewarding and the most life-enhancing of all human experiences. It is also the only one which both has a completely satisfying ending and yet can be endlessly repeated. Not even the greatest works of literature and music can stand such iteration. But this wonderfully enriching experience is only possible when the two people concerned have achieved a relationship in which, at least during the actual process of love-making, each is able to confront the other exactly as they are, with no reserves and no pretences, and in which there is no admixture of childish dependence or fear.

In this most intimate relation, we are all vulnerable, and we all reveal ourselves for what we are. So that if we are people who have been unable fully to emerge from childhood, our childishness will inevitably manifest itself in our sexual behaviour; and a sexual deviation can generally be understood in terms of the persistence of a childish kind of relation to the other person, or else as an attempt to overcome such a relation and so reach a greater degree of adult freedom.

Hesitancies and anxieties in relation to other people can generally be traced to the persistence of childhood patterns; above all to the persistence of the kind of emotional link which the child formed with its parents in its earliest years. If this was characterized predominantly by love and acceptance, the child will be likely to be able to achieve a mature sexual relationship without much difficulty; but if, for one reason or another, the child felt that it was not fully accepted and loved by its parents, it will probably find it difficult to achieve that full and free intimacy with another person which we have postulated as characteristic of a happy love relationship.

In discussing sexual deviation, we shall be discussing forms of relationship between persons which fall short of this ideal intimacy. For deviant sexual behaviour is the behaviour of those who have been, for varying reasons, unable to form relationships with the opposite sex on equal terms, and who cannot therefore give and receive love in a wholly satisfying way.

In the eyes of the general public, sexually deviant behaviour and criminal conduct are far too closely associated. Some newspapers devote a great deal of space to the detailed reporting of sexual offences, since their readers obtain vicarious erotic excitement from reading about such cases, especially about those rare instances in which force has been employed. The impression is thus created that sexual deviants are often violent criminals who roam the streets seeking victims upon whom to slake their perverted appetites. Nothing could be further from the truth. Most sexually deviant people are less assertive and less likely to be violent than their normal counterparts, and the majority never commit any offence which comes to the notice of the police. Of those sexually deviant persons who do commit offences, the majority are more nuisance than menace, since the offences which they commit are generally trivial. Contrary to popular supposition, there is no tendency for a man who has committed a trivial sexual offence to progress to committing more serious offences. Thus, although an exhibitionist may continue to expose himself, he is most unlikely to change the pattern of his behaviour and start to make assaults upon women. Moreover, more than eight in ten of those who are convicted of sexual offences have not previously been convicted of any offence at all; whilst those who have been previously convicted are at least as likely to have committed other, non-sexual offences. As one writer puts it: *I contend that burglary . . . is far more likely to be a forerunner of rape than homosexuality, voyeurism, exhibitionism, or any other type of sexual offence*; and the figures bear out his contention.

In other words, criminal conduct results from a general failure to control primitive impulses, whether these be sexual, violent, or simply the desire for easy money. Persistent sexual offenders do exist, but they represent only about three per cent of those who are convicted on sexual charges. By far the majority of sexual offences do not involve the use of force, and an examination of 1,994 victims of sexual offences showed that in ninety-one per cent there were no notable physical consequences.

It is impossible even to estimate the number of persons in our society who are sexually deviant, although it is obvious that the figure must be large. For most deviant people neither commit offences nor seek treatment; and no general survey designed specifically to elicit the prevalence of deviant impulses or practices has yet been undertaken.

There is a great need for more research into the origin and meaning of sexual deviations. It is clear that the seeds of most deviations are sown early in life, and that failure to reach sexual maturity can best be understood in terms of difficulties in the changing relation between the child and its parents. This is not to say that this is the whole explanation. There may well be genetic factors which contribute to the partial failure of the child to outgrow dependency and break away from parental ties. But it is impossible to explain the meaning and content of most sexual deviations in terms of inheritance. Some people believe that homosexuality may be due to a chromosomal aberration; but it could hardly be argued that a sexual interest in silk underclothing or red hair was the result of inborn factors rather than experience.

The most important thing is that we should strive to understand, rather than pass judgement. Seen through conventional eyes, sexual deviations may appear incomprehensible, disgusting, or ludicrous. They are often all these things in the opinion of those who suffer from them, which is one reason why they tend to persist; for it is always that which cannot be accepted or assimilated by the person as a whole which remains immutable. But to the eye of understanding, sexual deviation is a matter for compassion rather than condemnation or ridicule, and those who do no more than turn away from such things with a contemptuous shrug lay themselves open to the suspicion that they are turning away from something in themselves as well as being uncharitable. As we have already said, not one of us attains complete emotional maturity, and embryonic forms of sexual deviation can be discerned in everybody.

Deviant sexual behaviour is, like all human behaviour, extremely complex. It is true to say that all sexual deviations are forms of immaturity, childish attitudes which have not been outgrown; but it is also possible to detect in these immature forms of relationship strivings towards maturity, and even the most bizarre deviations have a compensatory aspect which contains a core of positive value. The descriptions and explanations which follow must be taken as tentative rather than authoritative. We are not yet sufficiently advanced in our subject to possess a psychopathology of universal application. But it is better to have some stated framework than none; for there then exists something which can be disputed; and without controversy progress is impossible. In the author's view, sexual deviations are chiefly the result of the persistence of childhood feelings of guilt and inferiority; and it is therefore to a discussion of these topics that the next two chapters are devoted.

2 Sexual Guilt

During the past fifty years society's attitude to sex has altered. There is far more open discussion of sexual problems than there used to be, and far more tolerance of the sexual interests and behaviour of children. This change in attitude may be traced to the work of Freud, whose demonstration of the facts of infantile sexuality provoked intense hostility at the beginning of this century, but whose views upon sexual development have since become widely accepted. In spite of this, however, many people continue to suffer from severe feelings of guilt concerning their sexual impulses, and this is especially characteristic of the sexually deviant. A sense of guilt about sex, which is often deeply embedded in the mind of a child, encourages the expression of deviant tendencies, for it acts as a dam which holds back the stream of normal development, forcing the sexual impulse into indirect and more tortuous channels. It may seem paradoxical that homosexual behaviour or voyeurism or other deviant acts are attended with less guilt than conventional heterosexuality, but such is actually the case with people who suffer from these deviations; for, in their eyes, it is the normal sexual act which is encompassed with fear and shame.

Since guilt is a crucial factor in the production of sexual deviation, it is important to discuss its origin. There can be little doubt that it is the attitude of the parents towards sex which most powerfully determines the child's acceptance or rejection of its own developing erotic feelings; and it is suggested later that some of this guilt is inescapable. But the attitude of society as a whole is also a potent influence in causing guilt, and this is particularly true of our own Western civilization, which is far less tolerant of sexuality than many cultures.

Sexual guilt is a burden from which few human beings can completely emancipate themselves in a society which is based upon supposedly Christian values, and over which hangs the shadow of hundreds of years of ecclesiastical disapproval. The obsessive preoccupation with details of sexual behaviour which characterized the medieval church is no longer with us; but it has left its mark upon the legal codes of both Britain and the United States which still contain anomalies and anachronisms deriving from ecclesiastical prejudice. So wide a range of sexual activities is officially proscribed that Kinsey calculated that, if the law were to be strictly enforced, no less than ninety-five per cent of the male population of the U.S.A. would be confined in penal institutions. It is not always appreciated that, even today, the orthodox Christian attitude towards sex is, when one considers the generality of mankind, exceptionally severe. As one anthropologist remarks, the Christian prohibition of all sexual relations outside marriage is characteristic of only a handful of human societies which include, at the most, not more than five per cent of the human race.

There is good reason to suppose that it is the man who can achieve a stable heterosexual partnership who is best able to love his neighbour as himself; but the idea that sexual abstinence is an expression of a superior morality, and that celibacy is to be equated with virtue is still widely held, especially by those who belong to churches which insist that their clergy shall not marry. Such beliefs, which have been current for centuries, die hard; and, even in a society which is only nominally Christian, and in which the church itself is becoming gradually more liberal in sexual matters, there are many people who still seem to suppose that sex is only another word for sin.

The most notable Christian attempt to break away from this attitude has been that of a group of Quakers, whose pamphlet *Towards a Quaker View of Sex* reflects an exceptionally sane and liberal spirit.

The attitude which society has towards sex affects us all, and no one can entirely escape the pressure of ideas which are generally held however violently he may disagree with them. Parents, by their behaviour, often convey to children attitudes which they would themselves repudiate, unaware that they are passing on collective patterns which have become deeply implanted. A parent, for instance, may freely be able to answer his child's questions about sex in private, but there are few parents who do not show some embarrassment when a child makes such inquiries in the presence of strangers. Collective prejudice is certainly one factor which contributes to sexual guilt and hence to sexual deviation; and although all societies place some restraints upon sexual conduct in order that the minimal protection of infants shall be ensured, there is little doubt that the attitude of our own Western society towards sex has been the source of much unnecessary distress and maladjustment.

A detailed comparison of the prevalence of true, compulsive sexual deviation in various societies would be a fascinating study; but it is one which is beyond the scope of this book and the competence of its author. In understanding the development of the individual, and more especially the development of sexually deviant people, it is still more valuable to consider how sexual guilt arises within the family.

We all start life as weak, helpless creatures, totally dependent for both our physical and mental well-being upon those who care for us. It has been demonstrated that, from the very beginning of its separate existence, the baby requires more than simple attention to its physical needs. If a baby is to develop satisfactorily, it is not enough merely to feed it and keep it warm; it needs a mother as a person who will play with it, caress it, and show it affection in all the hundred ways in which mothers do show love towards a child which has been desired and which is welcomed. Babies who are cared for physically, but whose emotional needs are neglected, develop more slowly and may, in some instances, suffer permanent damage in that, in adult life, they may never be able to form close emotional ties with any other human being. Every psychiatrist has seen examples of people who were brought up in institutions and who, perhaps, were excellently fed and clothed, but whose emotional needs were left quite unsatisfied. As a result, they grew up into a kind of person who can never keep a friend because the demands which they make upon others are not those of friendship, but rather those of a lost child looking for a parent who can never be found.

But even the child who is fortunate enough to have loving parents soon learns that their affection is not indiscriminately bestowed. Certain actions and behaviour evoke especial praise, whereas others call forth, if not condemnation, at least some lessening of enthusiasm. It is better to eat the food which is put before one than to throw it on the floor; it is better to use the pot than to wet the bed; it is better to be brave when one hurts oneself than to burst into tears. Obviously, every child learns such simple lessons by the gradual discovery of what pleases and what displeases his parents; and since, in the normal household, the love of his parents is what gives the child a sense of well-being and security, he soon learns to comply with parental wishes in so far as his instinctive nature will permit.

Very early indeed, standards of good and bad become introjected. That is, the small child swallows parental attitudes whole without questioning. Their bad becomes his bad; their good his good. It is only later that he will rebel against parental standards, and discover that not everyone has the same view of what is good and what is bad as obtained in his own household. Guilt is the emotion which he feels when he realizes that, within him, are desires and impulses which are 'bad' according to the standards which he has himself adopted. Such feelings make him insecure and lower his self-esteem, even when he is alone and there is no parental voice outside him to indicate disapproval.

There are various reasons why sex is apt to become particularly loaded with guilt. First, there is society's attitude, which, we have already suggested, has its effect on even the most individualistic of its members. Second is the fact that, whilst many parents have learned not to condemn the developing sexual interests and behaviour of their children, they seldom actually praise sexuality or say anything good about it. The mere absence of positive approval is, for the sensitive child, enough to label the subject as 'bad' and to create a sense of guilt about it. The gentle voice which suggests that playing with trains is better than playing with oneself may, for some children, be as effective a conditioning instrument as the slap or the angry word. Third, the process of toilet training, which gradually instils into the childish mind the notion that both the process of excretion and also its products are 'dirty', may create similar attitudes to sex. For the organs concerned with reproduction are either the same as, or contiguous with those which serve for excretion; and if an exaggerated sense of disgust is created about the one process, it is likely to extend to the other.

Clinical experience suggests that the majority of patients who seek help from a psychiatrist because of sexual deviations were, as children, particularly impressionable. Most of these people belong to the introverted or dysthymic type. They tend to be withdrawn and unsociable, to substitute thought for action, and, especially in the sexual sphere, to live in a world of phantasy which may be quite unrelated to any real possibility of sexual fulfilment. It has been shown experimentally that, in introverted people, conditioned reflexes are more easily established. It is not surprising, therefore, that the introverted child is often burdened with a more highly developed sense of guilt than his extraverted brother, since it is he who is the more susceptible to the influence of parental approval and disapproval. But it is facile to assume that sexual guilt arises only in this manner.

Since Freud made public the facts of infantile sexuality, emancipated parents have been at pains not to threaten castration, disapprove of masturbation, interfere with childish sexual games, or behave in the condemnatory fashion, which, it is supposed, was the standard practice of their Victorian forebears. Parents may conceal from their children neither their anatomy nor even the details of their own sexual lives; and yet, in spite of the apparent licence which has been allowed them, the children will feel guilt about sex and will want to conceal their own sexual behaviour.

To some extent guilt about sex is inevitable, however liberal and understanding the parents, for sex cannot normally find its full expression within the family circle. The so-called incest taboo precludes the satisfaction of even infantile sexuality, and so sex for the child is bound to remain partially a secret and thus something about which he feels some sense of guilt. For if within the child there are powerful impulses which cannot be brought into relation with those upon whose approval he is dependent, he is bound to feel guilty about these impulses, even if the parents do not show active disapproval. It may even be more difficult to escape from parents who appear to have been loving and kind than those who have been crudely moralistic. It is harder to rebel against love than against authority; and some children who carry into adult life an excessive load of sexual guilt are those who have not dared to differentiate themselves from parents who may seem to have been particularly understanding, but who have actually intensified the emotional relationship so that it becomes more difficult for the child to break it.

The taboo on incest regarded objectively is highly desirable. It is also sanctified by so long a history that its origins are lost in antiquity. Whatever the ultimate reason for man's condemnation of incest, except under such special circumstances as the preservation of a royal line or performance of a ritual, there can be little doubt that incest between parent and child is generally to be deplored. Owing to the long period of immaturity it is in any case difficult for children to emancipate themselves sufficiently from the emotional ties with their parents, especially in the close-knit, small, and exclusive families of our own society. No child gains independence without hesitations and struggles. If, to the manifold bonds of loving dependency, there is added the complication of an overt sexual involvement, the problem of winning adult freedom becomes so difficult that children who have experienced incestuous relations with their parents may never surmount it. Everyone knows the difficulty which a daughter may find in parting from a widowed father, or a son in leaving a mother who lives on her own. Where there is only one parent the emotional tie with a child of the opposite sex is always intensified, even if there is no physical expression of love. It is increased still further if the incest taboo is explicitly disregarded; and every psychiatrist has seen cases in which an incestuous relationship has prevented a child from later finding a suitable sexual partner.

It is because its sexual impulses cannot be satisfied within the normal family that the child is forced to look elsewhere for a mate. Sexuality thus becomes the main force which divides children and parents, and this is one reason why it becomes a focus of guilt. Parents may be well advised not to inquire too closely into their children's sexual lives; for it is necessary for children to have secrets if they are to become independent beings, and the child's developing sexual interests ought naturally to form the nucleus of its emancipation. A certain degree of sexual guilt, which is almost inevitable in adolescence, may, therefore, have its advantages, since it encourages the young person to look for others of his own age who will be more understanding towards him than his parents appear to be, for they will be able to accept his sexuality in a way which his parents can never do.

When adult status is finally achieved and a heterosexual partner has been won, sexual guilt ought, ideally, to disappear. A child who has been brought up in a happy home knows what it is to be loved, but the love which he experiences is always incomplete. It is only when he becomes a lover that he recognizes that sense of absolute completion, of total union, which results from being loved both body and soul.

Unfortunately, a sense of sexual guilt may be so extreme that the child is unable to overcome it and continues to carry it with him into adult life, with the result that his capacity for forming adult relationships is impaired. One consequence of this impairment is a tendency towards various forms of sexual deviation, which, as has been indicated above, can often be understood as a failure to outgrow the sexual interests and practices of childhood.

It has already been suggested that, on account of the incest taboo, some degree of sexual guilt is inescapable. In other words, the closer and more prolonged the emotional tie with the parents the more guilt is likely to persist. Guilt is not necessarily the product of specific parental prohibition, but rather may be one aspect of a child's unwillingness to leave the protective shelter of his parents' care. Sexual guilt and a general failure to become independent are opposite sides of a single coin. For to continue to feel guilty is to hold on to the taboo on sexuality which was felt by the child to have been imposed at home, and which, it has not yet fully realized, is not imposed *except* within the home. In some instances, sexual guilt may be the cause, in others the result of a prolongation of the dependence of childhood. The two disabilities invariably march hand-in-hand, and to say which precedes the other is generally impossible.

The more tied a man is to his parents, the more will he think of other people in terms of his parents, and the more will he unconsciously suppose that they are also likely to disapprove of his sexuality. And so the more will his sexuality find expression only in phantasy, and the less will it be related to actual people in the external world. Everyone, whether deviant or not, has some inclination towards dissociating the sexual aspects of other people from the rest of their personalities, and thus to imagine two categories of persons, those who are nothing but sexual objects, and those who show no sexuality at all. This happens in both men and women, but is especially obvious in the male, whose tendency to divide women into two groups, 'good' and 'bad', mothers and prostitutes, has often been remarked. The reason for this dissociation is ultimately to be traced to the incest taboo, which, by forbidding the mother as a sexual object, creates in the mind of the child the notion of a woman without sexuality. Traces of this idea are detectable in many normal people who can recall that, in childhood and adolescence, they found it hard to imagine their parents ever having sexual intercourse.

People with sexual problems, because of a persistent emotional tie with the parent of the opposite sex, generally show this tendency to split people into two categories very markedly. Sexual phantasy is often concerned with figures who are unrelated to real people, but are mere personifications of the erotic; and many sexual difficulties and deviations are related to the fact that the sufferer is unable to fall in love with a real person, but is emotionally bound to figures of his inner world who may be such that they are incompatible with actual persons.

For falling in love implies amongst many other things that a person can relate his inner world of phantasy to a real person in the external world and thus find, at any rate for a time, the greatest happiness known to man. It is only when the inner figure and the outer appear to coincide that the phenomenon of falling in love occurs, and that there is a complete correspondence between the sexual desires which the person has felt in phantasy and the desire which he now feels for an actual person. Falling in love is often marked by the disappearance of deviant phantasies and actions, for it is no longer necessary for the person to hold on to what has given pleasure in the past, since he is now absolutely assured of fulfilment in the present. But extreme sexual guilt prevents a person from falling in love, since he cannot believe that another will find acceptable what he himself has tried to reject.

Guilt always implies rejection and non-acceptance; and so long as it persists, so long will any sexual deviation to which it has contributed persist. In most cases it is only when the deviation can be assimilated and understood that the sufferer can progress beyond it, and this is why the relief of sexual guilt is generally such an important part of the therapist's task.

3 Sexual Inferiority

Guilt is one barrier which may be strong enough to prevent the child's developing sexuality from finding mature expression. A conviction of sexual inferiority is an impediment of equal importance. We saw, in the last chapter, that sexual guilt is, to some extent, inevitable; and that it is only when an unusually impressionable constitution or adverse family circumstances have exaggerated the guilt which every child is bound to feel, that he may encounter sexual difficulties. The belief or fear that one is less than adequately masculine or feminine is also ubiquitous.

Sexual confidence is popularly believed to depend upon physical beauty which, as Gibbon pointed out when writing of Mahomet, is 'an outward gift which is seldom despised, except by those to whom it has been refused'. No one doubts that good looks are a help to morale; but it is remarkable how low a correlation there may be between physical appearance and the person's own view of his or her desirability. A woman may be extremely beautiful, and yet not believe that she is lovable. Indeed, the possession of beauty, like that of wealth, is a doubtful asset when combined with inner uncertainty; for a beautiful woman may be gratified by admiration and yet feel that this is directed merely towards her appearance, and not towards herself as a person; just as the rich may be flattered by those who pursue them, and yet never be certain that it is their company rather than their wealth which makes them sought after.

The distinction between loved 'for oneself' and loved because one is physically attractive requires some explanation; for the idea that the essential core of a person is something discrete from his body is a sophisticated conception. It may be assumed that, at the beginning of life, there is no difference between being loved physically and loved as a person. The mother, handling and breast-feeding her baby, does not herself make any such distinction; and the infant can hardly be supposed to be conscious of a split between body and mind. It is probable that the basis of self-confidence in later life is this initial total acceptance, in which the baby is loved for its mere existence without anything being expected of it in return. In adult life, a lover may adore his beloved with an equally uncritical and irrational devotion, but during the long journey from babyhood to falling in love, the child will never again experience a love which is unconditional, nor one in which it is treated as a totality. For, as the child grows older, it is bound to become aware of the fact that the love of its parents is not all-inclusive. In the last chapter, it was pointed out that, on account of the incest taboo, parental love was always incomplete; for whereas more general embraces might be permitted, love between child and parent could not normally include the giving and receiving of the kind of sexual pleasure which is centred upon the genitals. As soon, therefore, as the child discovers that the genital organs are the chief source of physical delight, he must also become vaguely aware that there are two aspects of himself; that part which is loved by his parents, and which he will probably feel to be the more essential so long as he depends upon them, and that part which is excluded from their embrace, but which nevertheless gives him intense pleasure. In the last chapter it was suggested that one effect of the incest taboo was to encourage the child to divide persons into two groups, sexual and non-sexual. A second and similar effect is to encourage a split in the child's view of himself, so that he becomes, as it were, a non-sexual being in one set of circumstances and a sexual being in another, instead of feeling that his sexuality is an integral part of himself and his relation to others.

When he later matures sufficiently to break his ties with home and discover a mate, he will find that this split can be healed, and that he can once again be loved as a whole as he was in infancy.

Meanwhile, there is an interim period during which his body and his essential self are no longer felt to be identical, since his parents continue to love the latter, but to exclude the most important part of the former. From this distinction springs the idea that there can be a self without a body; and it is on this basis that a person can believe himself to be physically attractive without being lovable, or lovable without being physically attractive.

Confidence that one is, or can be, lovable is more essential than assurance in one's physical appeal. Although a high degree of physical attractiveness may lead to a succession of conquests, it does not enable a man or woman to achieve a sustained relationship unless it is supported by an underlying conviction of being valuable as a person. Many sexually attractive people who have no such conviction terminate a sexual partnership almost as soon as they have achieved it for fear that, if the relationship were to continue, the partner would discover that they were fundamentally unlovable and abandon them on this account. Continual promiscuity is not generally reckoned to be a sexual deviation; but it is equally a failure to achieve a mature sexual relationship. On the other hand, those who lack beauty, but who feel confident of their acceptability as persons, are generally able to make so close and deep a relationship with another that love finds its natural sexual expression in spite of their doubts about their own attractions.

It was stated above that a conviction of sexual inferiority was regularly to be found in people suffering from sexual deviation. From what has been said already, it will be seen that such a conviction has two roots. The first, and basically more important, is a generalized feeling of being unlovable which may often be attributed to an early failure in the relationship between child and mother. The second is a more specific inability to identify with the current role assigned by society to male or female.

To be totally confident as a man or a woman is a gift which is granted to so few that it seems doubtful whether such a state of mind can be said to exist. In Western civilization, there is evidence to suggest that very large numbers of people require repeated reassurance about their sexual role. Vance Packard in *The Hidden Persuaders* says:

The motivational analysts began finding that a major sexual need of both men and women in America at the mid-century was sexual reassurance. Women by the millions were yearning for evidence that they were still basically feminine and men by the millions were yearning for evidence that they were still indisputably and virulently masculine.

In the imagination of both advertisers and adolescents, the world is peopled by men and women of supreme sexual confidence. These fictitious figures look down on us from every hoarding, and stare at us imperiously from the pages of every glossy magazine. In this dreadful Utopia, lean, bronzed, athletic men stride through life with never a doubt about their masculinity, whilst their beautifully dressed women pose with the nonchalant elegance that demonstrates complete assurance in their feminine charms. Such men and women are never at a loss. Sophisticated, poised, serene, they confront both life and each other with the calm certainty that, in the eyes of the opposite sex, they are supremely desirable.

Real men and women were never like this; and the more intimately one becomes acquainted with even the most sexually successful of human beings, the more does one realize that Don Juans are little boys, that the highly promiscuous are incapable of love, and that the most ravishingly attractive exterior may conceal the profoundest inner uncertainty.

In those who become sexually deviant, a failure in identification with an adult sexual role is particularly pronounced. It may be that our present epoch is one in which it is unusually difficult for men and women to define and to feel confident in their respective sexual identities; and for this the effects of advertising, films, and television are partly to blame. Never before have so many people had held up to them the same sexual models with which to try to identify themselves, and in comparison with which they may feel inadequate. This sense of sexual inadequacy occurs in both men and women, but it is in the male that its effects are most clearly apparent. Although women can become sexually deviant in more than one way, the majority of the various types of sexually deviant behaviour are found only in the male, and are clearly related to the special need which men have to prove and to gain confidence in their masculinity. Why men seem to need more reassurance in their sexual role than women is related to three main factors. First, in the sexual act itself it is necessary for the man to achieve and sustain erection, whereas the woman can remain relatively passive. Second, in the process of development from child to adult, the male has to take an extra step of emancipation; for he has to become a creature quite different from the mother, whereas the girl can remain more closely identified with her. Third, as Margaret Mead maintains, there is no male equivalent to child-bearing, which, in the female, is the source of a deep and sustaining sense of success in the feminine role. Most societies have provided for the male's need for achievement by closing certain occupations to women and by emphasizing the importance of the activities which then become the prerogative of the male. As Margaret Mead remarks:

The recurrent problem of civilization is to define the male role satisfactorily enough, – whether it be to build gardens or to raise cattle, kill game or kill enemies, build bridges or handle bank-shares, – so that the male may in the course of his life reach a solid sense of irreversible achievement, of which his childhood knowledge of the satisfactions of child-bearing has given him a glimpse.

Until Huxley's 'Brave New World' has actually arrived, we may assume that women will retain their capacity for bearing children and that men will continue to be unable to emulate this particular creative activity. Are women, therefore, at an advantage in a society in which they are allowed to participate in practically every activity which was formerly confined to men and yet retain their special role as mothers? It does not seem so, if one can judge from the number of women who seem uneasy in their femininity. The emancipation of women has led to a society in which there is less differentiation between the parts which the two sexes are required to play, since, for most of the time, men and women do much the same things; and this has almost certainly resulted in a lessening of sexual confidence in both sexes.

The clock cannot be put back, and few would wish to deprive women of the opportunities of education and occupation which they have wrested from society with such difficulty. Nevertheless, the changed status of women in the West has presented society with a problem which, so far, remains unsolved: for, at the emotional level, the two sexes seem to make a better relationship with each other when their social roles are sharply differentiated in a way which reinforces the sense of sexual identity as man and woman.

These larger questions, must, however, be left to the historian and the sociologist. What we have to consider here is how, within the family, the child develops a sense of his or her sexual identity and how this process may go wrong in such a way that sexual deviation becomes a possibility.

The whole process of development can be seen as an attempt to discover one's own identity; and, since this cannot be done in isolation, the development of a person is conditioned by his relationship with other persons in all its extent. In this process, a changing kind of relationship occurs which may be concisely summarized by saying that a child progresses from being a passive, receptive creature, whose prime emotional contact with another is through the mouth, to a much more active creature who is able to give as well as receive, and whose most important contact with another is through the genitals. The intermediate stages of this progress are variously described by psychopathologists who do not always agree either in their concepts or in their terminology; but there is no real dispute about either the beginning or the end of emotional development. The attainment of maturity should include the disappearance of any lingering sense of being inferior to other adults in one's sexual nature. Ideally, the final stage is characterized not only by the genital organs taking pride of place as the channel of emotional communication, but also by the conviction in each sex of being lovable enough and adult enough to be able to give and receive love on equal terms with another adult.

It is difficult to say how early the child comes to realize to which sex it belongs. Some authorities maintain that there is an inborn awareness of sexual differences; a kind of foreknowledge which may even include very primitive images of the sexual organs. However this may be, the discovery that one parent is the same sex as oneself and that the other is different occurs very early; so early that most people cannot remember it. But to become aware of being anatomically boy or girl is a long way from what is meant by being identified with male or female in any adult sense. Every child begins life as part of the mother, and is therefore completely identified with her. Indeed, the realization of its separate existence from the mother comes only gradually to the baby, who at first seems unaware of even the boundaries of its own body. To be certain where one begins and ends, and of the relative size of the various parts of the body is an achievement, not an inborn condition; and the baby has to discover it just as a driver has to learn to sense the width of a new car when he first begins to drive it. The sense of identity, the feeling of being 'I' is rooted in the body, and may be lost in pathological conditions in which the boundaries of the body become blurred. This primary identification with the mother is replaced by a sense of separateness in which the mother is needed as an ever present protector of the child's tentative individuality. The small child begins to venture forth into the world as an independent being; but only from the secure base of the mother to whom it can quickly return if the world seems frightening.

By the time the child talks of itself as 'I' it will generally be aware of its own sex and will have already started the process of secondary identification. By this is meant the way in which the child models itself upon parents, brothers and sisters, teachers, and others who are close enough to be able to affect it emotionally. In learning to grow up, the child takes into itself characteristics of those around it; and in learning to be masculine or feminine it will normally be most affected by the parent of the same sex as itself. The process of identification with the parent of the same sex, which is essential for healthy development, is facilitated by a relationship which is affectionate and which is also continuous. Thus, a boy whose father is either absent or indifferent to him, has less chance of developing into a confident male than a boy whose father lives at home and is actively concerned with him. But even the latter may prove an inadequate example.

In very many cases of sexual deviation, it can be shown that a parent of the same sex had failed the child by being a deficient sexual model. A mother, for instance, who has never herself accepted her feminine role, may so undervalue femininity that her daughters find it difficult to be confident in their own. A father who is less than normally aggressive may inhibit his son's masculine development by failing to provide him with the notion that there are times when it is right for a man to fight, or at least to stand up for himself. Alternatively, a father may be so violent that he deters his sons from any attempt to be like him, and his daughters from intimacy with any man at all. There are innumerable ways in which parents can fail their children, some of which will be discussed in later chapters. Although it is possible for a child to learn how to be a man or how to be a woman from persons outside the family, it is the parents who provide the first and most penetrating impression. To develop its own identity as a sexual being, the child needs people whom it admires and whom it can imitate if its own potentialities are to be brought to full flower; and the inferiority feeling so characteristic of the sexually deviant can generally be shown to originate in an early failure in identification.

An extreme feeling of sexual inferiority means that the person concerned turns away from any attempt to be sexually competitive or even attractive. This has two results. First is the attempt to seek self-esteem in other ways than by being loved. Many sexually deviant people are for this reason intensely ambitious, and try to compensate for their inner sense of inferiority by achieving such power and success that they can compel respect and admiration even if they cannot command affection from their fellows.

The second result is to increase the importance of an inner world of phantasy. If a man cannot be convinced that he is sufficiently a man for a woman to love him, he will be driven in upon himself, and will only be able to find what he wants in his imagination. In the last chapter it was suggested that guilt was one factor which tended to increase sexual phantasy at the expense of real relationships. A sense of inferiority has the same effect. The sexual phantasies of a person who has been unable to make a happy heterosexual relationship have two main sources. One source is the actual erotic experiences of early childhood, which retain their emotional significance so long as nothing better arrives to replace them. The other is the natural tendency of the imagination to compensate for present lacks by constructing wish-fulfilling daydreams. As we shall see, the phantasies of the sexual deviant are usually compounded of elements which represent both past experience and future hopes together. The less a person has been able to relate himself to real people in the external world, the greater will be the tendency for him to imagine erotic situations of a totally impossible kind, in which sexuality is entirely separated from the rest of life and in which the figures which he conjures up have no personal characteristics other than their sexuality. The study of sexual deviation is very largely the study of sex divorced from love.

4   Sado-masochism

The term sadism is used to describe the sexual deviation in which erotic excitement is derived from the infliction of pain; the word masochism refers to the deviation in which sexual pleasure is aroused by its reception. The two words are often combined into one, since it has long been recognized that a person whose sexual interest is aroused by either activity is likely also to be stimulated by its opposite. A man or woman may be predominantly sadistic or masochistic in sexual tastes or behaviour; but it is usual to find the two attitudes combined, as they were in the people from whose names the terms are derived, the Marquis de Sade, and the Chevalier Leopold von Sacher-Masoch. De Sade was primarily concerned with domination and the infliction of pain; whereas Sacher-Masoch wished to be beaten and subjugated: but Sacher-Masoch could also be cruel, and de Sade had himself beaten as well as beating.

Both men were prolific writers, and both also showed evidence of other deviant impulses besides those for which they are famous. Sacher-Masoch had a fetishistic interest in fur, whilst de Sade was fascinated by sodomy; and it may be remarked in passing that sexual deviations are not mutually exclusive, but are often found combined in the same person.

In the first chapter it was suggested that the popularity of entertainments in which sexually-tinged violence played a part bore witness to the fact that sado-masochistic interests are widespread. This is further borne out by Kinsey's finding that more pornographic literature is especially devoted to sado-masochism than to any other type of sexual activity. It is certainly possible to detect sado-masochistic tendencies in everyone, and, as with other deviations, it cannot be said that there is any hard and fast line to be drawn between normal and abnormal.

The popular stereotype of the sadist as a brutal criminal applies to only a tiny minority of those in whom this deviant tendency is pronounced. There do exist violent, psychopathic characters like Neville Heath, who was executed for the murder of a girl whom he had first flogged; but the sadistic murderer is, fortunately, extremely rare. A very large number of people are, however, sexually excited to some extent by the idea of beating. Histories of corporal punishment can be found in every shady bookshop; and one such illustrated work which is on the shelves of a medical library in London has evidently been frequently consulted by the doctors who have access to it.

De Sade and Sacher-Masoch are not the only writers to exhibit this form of deviation. The poet Swinburne wrote a work entitled *Sadopaideia* which describes how an undergraduate was 'led through the pleasant paths of masochism to the supreme joys of sadism'; and his poem *Dolores* is an impassioned hymn to sado-masochism which contains some of his best-known lines.

> *Could you hurt me, sweet lips, though I hurt you?*
> *Men touch them, and change in a trice*
> *The lilies and languors of virtue*
>   *For the roses and raptures of vice;*
> *Those lie where thy foot on the floor is,*
>   *These crown and caress thee and chain,*
> *O splendid and sterile Dolores,*
>   *Our Lady of Pain.*

It is very characteristic of persons who are sado-masochistically inclined both to attempt to justify their interest, or to imagine that it could find fulfilment in some more tolerant age than the present. De Sade, in his political writings, advocated a future régime in which every citizen should be free to practise any deviation to which he was inclined; while Swinburne turned to

the past and imagines a pre-Christian era in which his own tastes
were accepted.

> *Thou wert fair in the fearless old fashion,*
> *And thy limbs are as melodies yet,*
> *And move to the music of passion*
> *With lithe and lascivious regret.*
> *What ailed us, O gods, to desert you*
> *For creeds that refuse and restrain?*
> *Come down and redeem us from virtue,*
> *Our Lady of Pain.*

The influence of sado-masochism can be detected in the writings of many other authors who do not admit, or perhaps even
recognize their inclination. It is impossible, for example, to read
the short stories of Conan Doyle, or the libretti of W. S. Gilbert,
without becoming aware that pain held something of a fascination for them; and even the poet Tennyson admitted an interest
in de Sade.

People who consult a psychiatrist on account of sado-masochistic impulses are, predictably, those who are ill-at-ease with
these impulses. There are many, however, who do not try either
to suppress their desires or to alter their direction; and those who
cannot find a willing partner in spouse or lover buy what they
want from prostitutes who keep a supply of whips, racks, mana-
cles, and other devices to comply with their clients' requirements.
It is rare to find either sadists or masochists who have inflicted or
received serious physical injury, although extensive bruising
occurs in a few instances, and the writer has seen one woman
who was alarmed by the severity of the damage which she had
herself invited from her lover. Proust's description of the chaining
and flogging of M. de Charlus in a Parisian brothel does not
exceed what may sometimes actually occur; but the majority of
the sado-masochistically inclined, in acting upon their impulses,
do not go beyond comparatively mild forms of beating. Phantasy,
however, has no limits; and in de Sade it is possible, though
rapidly tedious, to read of tortures and murders galore. De Sade
spent much of his life in prison; but his physical confinement did

not have the effect of restraining his imagination, and, in his phantasies, he makes no attempt to conform to the limitations of reality.

To the civilized eye, nothing appears more incongruous with love than the desire to hurt or be hurt; but, at a physiological level, all human passions are closely linked, and love and pain are less disparate than liberal humanists may like to think. The behaviour of people who are in the throes of sexual excitement is indistinguishable from that of people in severe pain. As Kinsey says: *In the most extreme types of sexual reaction an individual who has experienced orgasm may double and throw his body into continuous and violent motion, arch his back, throw his hips, twist his head, thrust out his arms and legs, verbalize, moan, groan, or scream in much the same way as a person who is suffering the extremes of torture.*

Freud's discovery that a small child who witnessed sexual intercourse between adults was likely to interpret it as an attack by the man upon the woman is scarcely surprising. It is to be expected that an encounter so passionate would be associated with violence and hurt in the mind of a child whose experience of coming up against other bodies in a forceful way has hitherto been only painful. For sexual intercourse is the only habitual human activity in which two bodies can be forcefully engaged *without* causing pain to one another. We all interpret the unfamiliar in terms of the familiar; and some children who discover that beating or other sado-masochistic practices such as tying each other up are sexually exciting, are undoubtedly substituting an activity which is known and comprehensible to them for one which is still mysteriously remote from their actual experience. Such interests persist in those who, because of sexual inferiority or guilt, have been unable to make a mature love-relationship; so that the sado-masochistic practice or phantasy carries the emotional charge which is felt by the normal person to belong to sexual intercourse.

Some of those for whom sado-masochistic practices have a peculiar fascination seem to be trying to reach an intensity of sexual experience of which they have an inner imaginative picture but which they cannot find in love-making unaccompanied by painful stimuli. In such people there is an internal embargo on the passionate aspect of love, so that love-making is too gentle and too tender to be wildly exciting. Paradoxically, the sado-masochistic person is often over-anxious not to hurt or to be hurt by his partner, and so may be less than normally forceful or yielding in the act of love. The sado-masochistic phantasies and actions which attract him are compensations for this lack of passion – ways in which he can reach the intensity of erotic experience which other, less inhibited men reach naturally during the sexual act.

It is only when sado-masochism is extreme or divorced from sexual intercourse that it can be counted a deviation. For countless couples engage in minor sado-masochistic rituals which serve the purpose of arousing them erotically, and are thus valuable introductory steps to the sexual act itself. Are there any two lovers who have not played some version of the age-old game in which one dominates and the other submits, or who have not teasingly tormented each other by pretending to kiss and then withdrawing? Such games may seem remote from the floggings of a de Sade or the humiliations of a Sacher-Masoch, but both spring from the same fundamental roots.

Although it may be semantically accurate to restrict the term sado-masochism to relationships in which actual pain is given or received, it is generally accepted that the concept has a wider connotation. Many relationships which do not include physical pain are essentially sado-masochistic. The adjective may justifiably be applied to any form of interpersonal relationship in which aggressive behaviour, verbal or physical, is a prominent feature, or in which one partner is markedly dominant and the other notably submissive. Although it is common for pain to form a part of such relationships, it is not the essential feature, and may be absent altogether. Comprehended in this wider sense, sado-masochism can be seen to enter into almost every human relationship which falls short of our ideal of maturity – the ability to give and receive love on equal terms – and it is certainly a most important and basic aspect of many sexual deviations which may not, at first sight, seem to be either sadistic or masochistic in themselves. Many forms of fetishism for instance, contain a sado-masochistic component; and the exhibitionist, in his desire to shock or horrify, can reasonably be said to be behaving sadistically towards those to whom he exposes himself. It is the desire to be either omnipotent or totally subjugated rather than the wish to give or receive pain which is the fundamental root of this deviation. In this connexion it is interesting to record that de Sade wrote in his novel *Aline and Valcour* the following passage, which is said to be autobiographical:

Allied through my mother with all the grandeur in the kingdom, and connected through my father with all that was most distinguished in Languedoc – born in Paris in the heart of luxury and plenty – as soon as I could think I concluded that nature and fortune had joined hands to heap their gifts on me. This I thought because people were stupid enough to tell me so, and that idiotic presumption made me haughty, domineering and ill-tempered. I thought everything should give way before me, that the entire universe should serve my whims, and that I merely needed to want something, to be able to have it.

As an example of the opposite attitude, I quote (with permission) from the phantasies of a modern masochist.

I like to imagine any group of men or women being led into slavery. Slave markets. Being stripped naked, examined as animals. Being sold, having a master to work for or submit to sexually ...

A master is superior to God because he exists in the flesh. A slave realizes that he is significant only so far as he is perfectly submissive. He delights in his status as slave and loves seeing others enslaved. Two chief moments of pleasure in the fantasies. 1. The moment of enslavement. Free one minute, slave the next. This is the recurring importance of the slave market scenes. I ought to add that in my mind it has a kind of poetic beauty. 2. The moment they are possessed by their master. Their life had been empty and without meaning, frivolous and trivial. Now it is exactly the opposite.

A slave has no past, he has no name. A master is beyond criticism, whatever he does or orders is immensely significant, he is incapable of evil or wrong, he cannot insult or degrade a slave. He can only honour him by noticing him. The only relationship the slave fears is that of friendship. This would be against nature and shatter his world.

Domination versus submission; freedom versus slavery; absolute power versus absolute helplessness – these are the opposites which constitute the basis of sado-masochism, and to which any preoccupation with pain is secondary. In order to understand how it is that adult human beings can be enthralled by such ideas it is necessary to examine the development of the so-called aggressive impulse in the child.

There has been considerable argument amongst psychopathologists about man's aggression, some maintaining that it is simply a response to frustration, others that it is an innately destructive drive which is directed against the self or against the external world. There is as yet no general agreement upon this fundamental point; but this need not inhibit our discussion, since the manifestations of aggression are recognized by all analysts, although they may disagree about its ultimate origin. Aggression can best be regarded as that aspect of psychic energy which subserves the differentiation of the individual as individual. That is, it is the drive underlying self-assertion, the desire for power, and the wish to be a separate person in one's own right. It is a fundamental aspect of human nature; and those people in whom aggression has been severely repressed are crippled as personalities and sometimes complain that they have no separate existence, but are nobodies, living in the shadow of other people. It can be assumed that, from the very beginning of life, there is present a drive towards self-realization, towards the finding of one's own identity as a person, and that this is a motive force as powerful as sex itself. It is characteristic of small children to be particularly concerned with asserting themselves, and a great part of the phantasy life of childhood is shot through with the desire to be big, to be strong, and to be master of the situation. Indeed, the further back one pursues the phantasy life of childhood the more aggression does one find, until, as Melanie Klein maintains, one reaches the intensely destructive, biting phantasies which can be deduced to underlie the oral activities and the rages of babies.

All children start life in a prison of which the gaolers are the parents, whether they be indulgent or severe; and all children have a drive to break the prison walls, and to overcome those who hold them captive. If children had no aggressive drive they would never become independent, never progress beyond a stage of being helpless, dependent, and restricted. They do not, of course, realize that it is their own dependent weakness which forms the walls of the prison; but attribute this to parents and other authorities, which seem to the child to be much stronger than is in fact the case. Growing up is as much a matter of realizing the weakness of others as of recognizing one's own strength. Indeed, it is a sign of adult wisdom to realize that no man is so strong that he can be totally independent. But, together with the wish to be free goes the desire to be loved, to be enclosed, to be protected. All children suffer this ambivalence, this Janus-faced looking backwards as well as forwards, and no adult is completely free from it either.

Those who are slow to mature or who, through the circumstances of their childhood, have never been able to develop, carry with them into adult life an exaggerated amount both of aggression and dependency. Such people relate to those they love as does child to parent, at least in the intimacy of the sexual relation, in which a person is perhaps revealed as he really is as in no other situation in life. In order to reach that freedom and confidence which is necessary for successful love-making, such people feel that they must either dominate their partner or themselves be dominated, and this is the origin of what we call sado-masochism.

For, in either situation, the person who is not wholly at ease with his partner feels safer. In the one he has proved himself strong enough to dominate and thus is superior. In the other, he has the satisfaction of being passively cared for, and so does not have to be independent. In other words, sado-masochistic relationships are re-creating childish patterns in which one partner is acting the child while the other is assuming the role of parent. But this is not a simple equation of dominance with parenthood and submissiveness with childhood. Both sadists and masochists begin by treating the partner as being unusually powerful. For someone who has to be forced into submission is almost as strong as someone to whom one has to yield. In neither case is there a sense of equality or of willing cooperation.

The anatomical difference between the sexes, and the act of coitus itself necessitates active penetration on the part of the male, whereas the female can remain relatively passive. There is thus some correlation between masculinity and sadism, and femininity and masochism. It is interesting that Kinsey records that women, who are sexually responsive to a far narrower range of stimuli than men, are frequently intensely aroused by being bitten; and Freud, in his early view of aggression, postulated that a certain sadism was necessary in the male in order to achieve conquest of the female.

Analogies from animal behaviour are always risky, but it is interesting to note that in certain fish

the only sexual difference in behaviour consists of the fact that three drives – sex, aggression and fear – which are always activated simultaneously when two strange fish meet, can be mixed in different ways in males and females. In the males just about every possible mixture and superposition of sexual and aggressive behaviour elements can be made, but the flight drive, even when minimal, will immediately inhibit the sexual drive. In the female, however, flight behaviour can mix very easily with sexual behaviour, whereas aggressiveness immediately suppresses sexuality.

It is probably true that men are generally more 'sadistic' and women more 'masochistic'. In clinical practice, at any rate, it is not very uncommon to find intensely masochistic women who desire to be subjugated, beaten, and ill-treated before they can be fully erotically aroused: but it is rare to find women who actually want to beat or ill-treat men in order to obtain erotic satisfaction. A woman who behaves aggressively towards men is generally either frightened so that she feels compelled to attack, or else is trying to force the man to overpower her by provoking him. Women in top boots cracking whips are generally either creatures of the masochistic male's imagination, or else prostitutes obliging their clients by trying to fulfil their phantasies. But there are many women who nag unmercifully in the hope that their man will finally treat them with the force that they find exciting. Women who do have truly sadistic desires are more commonly identifying themselves with men, and, if they act upon such feelings, will therefore generally experience them in terms of a Lesbian relationship.

Men, however, though very commonly sadistic, are often masochistic as well; and this is because the inferior, or masochistic position is one which is shared by both sexes in childhood, and from which the woman need never emerge, although the man must do so if he is to become fully masculine.

It was asserted above that sexual deviations in general resulted from the persistence into adult life of childhood feelings of guilt and inferiority. This is particularly obvious in sado-masochism, for sadistic behaviour has the effect of relieving a sense of inferiority, whereas masochism has the result of assuaging feelings of guilt.

In both sexes, masochism characteristically combines pleasure and permission with humiliation and punishment. As can be seen from the phantasies quoted above, the masochist wishes to take no responsibility for himself and his sexuality, but to hand himself over to an authority. The master or mistress takes charge; and so the masochist can regress to a childish level at which he no longer has to make decisions or conscious choice. The authority, by punishing him, relieves his sense of guilt, and at the same time stimulates him erotically. (At one preparatory school the boys' name for beating was in fact 'stimulation'.)

Masochistic desires sometimes only become compulsive when the person concerned is depressed. Such a person is asking for punishment in order to restore his self-esteem, and, after its administration, feels that his sin has been expiated. This makes it possible for him to sin again, and thus repeat the pattern. The authoritarian figure who arouses desire and punishes at the same time is, in effect, giving permission for eroticism, although ostensibly disapproving of it. Pornographic literature is full of phantasies of stern, authoritarian women beating or making slaves of men; and such figures solve the masochist's problem of how to obtain sexual pleasure without feeling guilty about it, for they combine within themselves the erotic enticement of a mistress together with the authoritarian function of a parent.

Girls also frequently have phantasies of being beaten which later develop into phantasies of being raped. The idea of being forcibly overpowered by a male must have occurred to every woman at some time, although not all women recognize that the apprehension to which such thoughts give rise is not unmixed with pleasure. The situation of being overpowered by a male is also one in which permission is given to be erotic, since the victim is forced to comply. Thus she 'cannot help it', and can enjoy the thrill without incurring either blame or responsibility.

One further aspect of masochism needs to be mentioned. A sexual situation in which one partner is markedly dominant may be one which makes the other partner feel safe to abandon control over his impulses. One feature of sexuality which the immature find frightening is that, in order to experience full orgasm, it is necessary to lose ego-control. That is, a person is bound to 'let go' at some point, to let something happen to him rather than be in control of the situation. People who are timid and anxious find this very difficult, and generally show it in other ways besides the sexual. For example, people who cannot let go may tend to suffer from constipation because they cannot relax their bowel; from muscular aches and pains because they cannot relax their muscles; and may not be able to vault, to dive, or even to turn head over heels, since all these activities are ones in which one has at some point to take the plunge and relinquish conscious control.

Sexual activity to be satisfying must reach a point at which the ego abrogates its authority; and it may be easier for some people to do this if they feel that there is an external authority present who will control them even if they no longer control themselves. It is safe to let go if an authority permits it, and so the masochistic person, in addition to seeking relief of guilt, is also looking for a situation in which he can be sexual and yet be safe; and he does this by letting the other person control the whole situation.

The sadist, on the other hand, feels compelled to be intensely dominant before he can achieve sexual release. The masochist gives over the situation to the partner; the sadist refuses the partner any say in the situation at all. At the back of this desire to be intensely dominant is an inner feeling of weakness for which the sadism is a compensatory phenomenon. The sadist cannot afford to let his partner have any power, for then he might himself be hurt, castrated, or overwhelmed. In dealing with persons of whom one is frightened, one can either submit completely to them and thus disarm them, as do certain animals when they are faced with an opponent which they feel will be too strong for them; or one can make sure that they are so disarmed and disabled that they cannot do any harm. The sadist chooses the latter alternative.

Sadism, as we have stated, extends far beyond the actual giving of pain; and many sadistic phantasies are really concerned with rendering the partner helpless and at the mercy of the attacker. In pornographic literature, therefore, it is common to find lengthy accounts of tying people up, chaining them, gagging them, and so on. But the desire to render a sexual partner helpless is not confined to the obviously sexually deviant. Traces of similar impulses are universal, and one has only to turn to the study of costume to detect them. The Chinese practice of foot-binding, hobble skirts, and other intensely restricting fashions bear witness to the eagerness with which man welcomes the crippling of his women, and to the submissiveness with which women will follow many fashions which are certainly uncomfortable, and sometimes actually painful.

By rendering his partner helpless, the sadist is creating a situation in which he feels free to do anything he likes to her, whether she wants him to or not. In other words, the sadist has no conception that his partner might invite or welcome his sexual activities. He cannot believe that anyone can really accept him sexually, and thus has to obtain by force what other more confident men expect to be given freely. It is only when he has established complete ascendancy over his partner that the sadist can hope for sexual fulfilment; for it is only then that the partner is no longer frightening. Erotic stories exist in which recalcitrant wives have to be sent to establishments in which they are educated to submit to their husbands' desires. In this phantasy world, they are beaten and humiliated and, at the same time, taught to be erotically skilful; so that, on their return home, they are anxious to please their husbands, and have learnt to enjoy the pleasures of slavish submission to a dominant male.

For the sadist, in spite of his apparently aggressive attack on the object of his desire, is actually anxious that she shall enjoy the pain or humiliation which he inflicts. His prime desire is not to hurt but to establish ascendancy, and the beatings and other cruelties are ritual devices to create a situation in which erotic fulfilment is possible, rather than attacks which are designed to hurt. One of the principal difficulties which both the sadist and the masochist encounter is to find anyone whom they can believe will really enjoy the only situation in which they themselves find release. This is why persons who suffer from these deviations so often have recourse to prostitutes, who will at least simulate pleasure, and can be counted upon not to shun or turn away in disgust from procedures which an unsophisticated girl will generally condemn.

5

Fetishism

The word fetish was originally applied to inanimate objects worshipped by primitive peoples which were believed by them to possess magical qualities. From this the meaning was extended, according to the *Shorter Oxford English Dictionary*, to connote 'something irrationally reverenced'.

A person in love may be said to treat his beloved as if she had magical qualities, and to revere her irrationally; but he is not on this account a fetishist. The term fetishism is applied to a sexual deviation in which magic appears to reside, not in a whole person, but in a part of the person, an object connected with the person, or a symbolic substitute for the person. The fetishist feels a compulsive and irrational sexual attraction towards an inanimate object such as a glove or shoe; or is fascinated by some part of the body other than the genitals such as the hair or breast. In some instances deformity or damage to the body may be a focus of attraction, as in a case known to the writer in which a man was erotically aroused by boys who were crippled and had to wear leg-irons. More rarely, a particular action performed by a person becomes a sexual stimulus which is equivalent to a fetish; and cases have been reported in which smoking or coughing has come to be associated with sexual arousal.

Fetishism is a deviation which is almost entirely confined to the male sex, for reasons which will be discussed below. It is only a true deviation where the fetish is totally substituted for the person. Most fetishists are heterosexual, but homosexual fetishism also exists. In addition to the man mentioned above who was attracted by boys who wore leg-irons, the writer has seen a male homosexual in whom corduroy trousers were a fetish, and another to whom blond hair was of particular emotional significance. For many homosexual males, the penis itself becomes a fetish; a phenomenon which will be further discussed in the chapter on male homosexuality. Minor degrees of fetishism can be detected in every man, and there is no point at which one can say that normality ends and pathology begins. For any special feature of a woman upon which a man's erotic attention is focused may, in a sense, be called a fetish. Where this feature is a part of the body, the breast or the hair, for example, some writers have called the condition 'partialism'; but this is to introduce an unnecessary term into a subject already overloaded with jargon. A fetish may be an undergarment, a piece of jewellery, a particular kind of material, or a part of the body. In each case it is either a substitution of a part for a whole, so that the fetish attracts the emotion which would normally be directed towards a complete person; or else it arouses the same feelings which, in the ordinary man, are evoked by the female genitals.

That some degree of fetishism is ubiquitous is evident from the study of feminine fashion. Fashion depends upon shifting erotic interest from one part of the body to another; so that at one time the breast, at another the waist, and at another the leg becomes the chief focus of erotic interest – the part to which the masculine eye is first drawn; a part, therefore, which symbolizes the totality of the person.

During the past twenty years the female breast has been a universal fetish for the American male, and actresses who have little else to recommend them, have, through the possession of an unusually prominent bosom, achieved an ephemeral fame. During the twenties and thirties of this century, the female leg, which had only recently emerged from the long skirts which used to conceal it, was the principal feminine allurement; whereas, throughout most of the nineteenth century, the waist and sometimes the hips were the aspects of woman most emphasized by fashion. The tendency for eroticism to be selectively directed is universal and not confined to fetishists.

In so-called normal people, the garments or parts of the body which, in the deviant, are likely to become fetishes, serve to attract attention and to arouse interest – an interest which, especially if reciprocated, soon extends to include the whole person with particular emphasis upon the genitals. In the fetishist this extension is blocked; and so his interest stops short at, and becomes focused upon the fetish, which for him comes to have the significance which pertains to the person as a whole or to the genitals in the more normal individual. Instead of his erotic interest spreading, it remains obsessively fixed upon the part aspect of the person which happens to appeal to him.

It is usual to find that the fetish has its origin in very early childhood; and much was made of this fact by pre-Freudian writers, who conceived of fetishism as a kind of conditioned reflex. Thus, if a child had, accidentally, been erotically aroused by the feel of his mother's silken dress, by the sight of his sister's underclothes, or by the touch or smell of the rubber sheet which lay under him in his cot, it was supposed that he might remain for ever sensitized to one of these particular objects, and would therefore invariably demand its presence as a *sine qua non* of erotic excitement.

It can be shown experimentally that different types of people vary as to how easily they are conditioned. Extraverted persons form conditioned reflexes with difficulty, whereas, as was mentioned in Chapter 2, the introverted, dysthymic type requires less time and fewer applications of the stimulus for a conditioned response to be established. Fetishists and other sexual deviants tend to be introverted people who have a rich phantasy life, but who are often ill-adapted both to their fellow-men and to the realities of the external world. It is probable that their tendency to be easily conditioned plays a part in their deviation, and this may be the 'psychic factor of unknown origin' to which Freud refers in *Three Essays on the Theory of Sexuality* when he finds it necessary to assume 'that these early impressions of sexual life are characterized by an increased pertinacity or susceptibility to fixation in persons who are later to become neurotics or perverts'.

Moreover, the fact that fetishism is almost entirely confined to the male may also be related to the process of conditioning. For, as Kinsey has shown, the human male is sexually responsive to a far wider range of stimuli than the female, and seems also to be more easily conditioned by these stimuli. In general, women tend to be indifferent to sexual stimuli which do not include either physical caresses or an element of romance. They may enjoy reading sentimental novels and respond to amorous films; and they often become easily aroused by touch. But women do not, as do men, become excited by pornography, by erotic pictures, by nudity or physical display, or by a variety of other sexual stimuli which appeal to the visual sense and to the erotic imagination. There are no striptease shows for women, for very few women are aroused by such performances.

But the fact that to be male and to be introverted renders a person more liable to fetishism cannot be regarded as an adequate explanation of the phenomenon, for very many men can recall being erotically aroused in childhood by various stimuli, and yet do not remain obsessively attached to one trigger, as does the fetishist. It is necessary to postulate other factors as well.

The psychoanalytic explanation of fetishism is in terms of the castration complex – a basic, aboriginal fear which can be detected in every one of us, but which, it is supposed, is particularly emphasized in the fetishist. The castration complex is one of the corner-stones of psychoanalysis; an explanatory concept which finds almost as wide an application as the Oedipus complex itself. Freud originally described it in terms which seem too literally restricted to do justice to a complex which is thought to underlie so many of the fears and uncertainties which afflict humanity. Freud pictures a small boy who, through the experience of infantile masturbation, has already learned to value his penis highly; but who lives in fear of losing it on the grounds that his parents disapprove of his sexual activity. When he discovers that there are beings known as females who have no penises his worst suppositions are confirmed. For he interprets this feminine deficiency as the result of active interference rather than as a natural difference between the sexes; and his terror that he might be deprived of his own precious organ is thus reduplicated. Freud concluded that the fetishist was so especially terrified of castration that he was compelled to pretend to himself that women really had penises in spite of his knowledge that they did not; and that the fetish acted as a reassurance by representing the missing female penis. Freud supported this theory by pointing out that the fetishist invariably showed an aversion to the female genitals, and that some fetishes conceal this dreaded sight. 'Velvet and fur reproduces – as has long been suspected – the sight of the pubic hair which ought to have revealed the longed-for penis.' 'The underlinen so often adopted as a fetish reproduces the scene of undressing, the last moment in which the woman could still be regarded as phallic.' However, Freud continues: 'But I do not maintain that it is always possible to ascertain the determination of every fetish.'

Not many analysts would now think of the castration complex in the literal terms in which Freud first conceived it; although one may still find children whose parents have threatened to 'cut it off' and who may perhaps have been alarmed by their first sight of a naked female. As W. H. Gillespie, a distinguished psychoanalyst, says in a recent paper:

Ever since the analysis of Little Hans Freud stressed the fateful conjunction for a little boy of an external castration threat for masturbation with the observation of female genitals, leading the boy to the conclusion that castration really may happen to him. Now few will be disposed to deny that such experiences may have an important crystallizing effect and may give conscious form and expression to the fear; but as a full explanation for such a dominating and far-reaching anxiety Freud's theory seems to depend too much on accidental and external factors, too little on endopsychic ones.

There can be no doubt that Freud was right in interpreting the fetish as a reassurance; and, if the fear of castration is taken as a concise phrase which can be stretched to include all the fears which a man may have in connexion with the sexual act, it is legitimate to think of the fetish as a reassurance against castration. But it is doubtful whether every fetish is a substitute for a female penis, although this may be a possible interpretation in some instances.

Viewed from a slightly wider angle the situation becomes more comprehensible. The fetishist, like all sexually deviant people, suffers from inner feelings of sexual guilt and sexual inadequacy. This tends to make him excessively anxious in any sexual situation, with the result that, consciously or unconsciously, he fears impotence. (It is not disputed that, at one level, this fear of impotence may be due to a fear of castration.) So he creates a situation in which he is sure that he will be potent; and what more certain than something which he knows has served to arouse him in the past. The fetish, which became established as a sexual stimulus in early childhood, is not discarded in favour of a whole person, as it is in normal people, for the fetishist needs it as a thing upon which he can rely to produce an erection. He cannot necessarily be sure that a woman will do this, since, to him, a woman is still in some sense a frightening figure, and thus an inhibitor of erection as well as an arouser of desire. (Traces of this fear account for the common phenomenon of impotence when a man first attempts intercourse with a new partner.) In this way the fetish acts as a reassurance – a defence against fear, a magical device which ensures potency.

Women have no need of fetishes because they do not have to achieve or sustain an erection. The fears from which they suffer and which may impair their sexual enjoyment and performance are equally important, but they do not include this specific difficulty; and it is probably this fact, combined with the greater responsiveness of men to visual and other sexual stimuli which accounts for the latters' near monopoly of fetishism.

Freud considers that the fetish represents a female penis. Other psychologists have held different views. Hadfield, for example, says: *In all cases of fetishism we have analysed, the fetishistic object proved to be a breast substitute: for the breast is the first loved object of the infant, even before the mother herself becomes so.* The common factor in each explanation is the reassurance which the fetish gives, and the way in which it enables a man who is frightened of the opposite sex and uncertain of his masculine potency to overcome his fears. One example which supports Hadfield's view is of a man who came to an out-patient department with the complaint that he had a compulsive attraction towards jewellery, especially bangles. He had had a vicious and neglectful mother, and as a small child frequently went to bed feeling miserably unhappy. But he found that if he took one of his mother's bangles to bed with him, he felt more at peace; and he stole one from her dressing-table which he kept for some years. In adult life he liked his girl-friends always to wear bangles.

This example demonstrates the early origin of the fetish, and shows that it was originally used as a substitute for the mother in the way which Hadfield suggests. We may assume that the small boy found it erotically exciting as well as comforting; for we know that children who are neglected generally masturbate more than children who are loved. The bangle, therefore, became an object which was both reassuring and which also could be counted upon to produce an erection. A boy whose mother is neglectful and harsh will almost certainly have difficulty in falling in love when he grows up, for he will expect other women to treat him as did his mother. He will be frightened that women will not like him, and frightened that he will be inadequate to their needs. It is not surprising that such a man holds on to the object which gave him reassurance in childhood, and that he feels more confident if a woman associates herself with it by wearing it.

The fetish also represents a symbolic break-through of the fetishist's defences. For, in such a person, sexual desire is so surrounded by guilt that it has been largely repressed. The fetishist has turned away from the body of the opposite sex, especially, as Freud observed, from the genitals.

The fetish replaces the genital difference between the sexes as a focus of interest. It is thus a triumph of displacement and a triumph of the human imagination. One can hardly imagine that an animal could become a fetishist, although, as Lorenz has shown, animals can become conditioned to sexual stimuli which are remote from those to which they might be expected to respond naturally.

In some examples, it seems probable that the fetish represents the female genitals, since the fetishist feels towards the fetish the same excitement and fascination which is aroused by the genital organs in the normal male. It is true that many men are frightened of penetrating the female, and regard the vagina with alarm; but this is not necessarily because the female is looked upon as a castrated male in the way in which Freud described. The female genital can itself be regarded as a castrating organ, as the myths of a *vagina dentata* attest. That is, a man may be frightened of penetrating a woman because women are still regarded by him as dangerous creatures who will damage him. For a man, the act of intercourse implies trusting a woman; for, in it, he is giving her power over his most tender and vulnerable part. If he is still in a stage of development where women are unconsciously treated more as mothers than mistresses, it is dangerous to have sexual intercourse, not only because of the incest taboo, but also because the woman is potentially stronger and therefore a threat as well as an enticement. The fear of the damage which she might do him is expressed as a fear of the female genital. Some fetishes serve the purpose of providing a focus of erotic excitement which is not the female genital and thus form a less alarming substitute.

Fetishes tend to be feminine symbols; objects which generally or exclusively pertain to the female sex, and which stand for femininity as a whole. Often they are garments which accentuate secondary sexual characteristics, such as brassieres, tight skirts, and high-heeled shoes. A fetish may, as it were, be a flag hung out by the woman to proclaim her sexual availability; and the man who demands that a woman should wear a particular garment is often asking that she shall, by this device, prove to him that she is a mistress and not a mother. Many men prefer their girl-friends to use every possible device to accentuate their sexual charms, often to the point of looking like prostitutes: and this masculine demand is really a plea for reassurance, a demonstration that sex is permissible and a proof of sexual accessibility. Once again, there is no demarcation between normal and abnormal, for, as Donne puts it, *Who forbids his beloved to gird in her waste? to mend by shooing her uneven lameness? to burnish her teeth? or to perfume her breath?* If a man's demand that his girl shall use some particular feminine device is to be regarded as abnormal, then no man can escape this censure.

Many fetishes, as has already been pointed out, have a sado-masochistic significance. The history of feminine fashion is full of devices which not only accentuate female sexual characteristics, but also restrict movement to the point of discomfort, if not of actual pain. The high-heeled shoe, which is probably the commonest fetish of all, is one example of this. Impractical, uncomfortable, highly restrictive, it shortens the stride, makes walking any distance impossible, and needs frequent repair. Nevertheless, high heels are such a potent weapon in the feminine armoury of devices to attract men that the structure of aeroplanes and the floors of great buildings have to be modified so that women may continue to wear them without doing too much damage. Many feminine fashions are apparently designed to make women appear more fragile and helpless than they actually are; and this appeals to men because it puts them in the superior position – one in which they can be protective, dominant, and physically more active. As was suggested earlier, the sadistic desire to have a helpless sexual object is latent in every man, and the masochistic desire to be at the mercy of a dominant lover can be found in every woman.

When the fetish absorbs the major part of a person's sexual interest he may go to extraordinary lengths to pursue it. Some fetishes are very hard to find; and if a man is unfortunate enough to be obsessed with something uncommon, for instance, a particular shade of red hair, it may be impossible for him to satisfy his desire except in phantasy. Indeed, it is true to say of all deviations that they are never fully satisfactory in reality; certainly never as satisfying as the normal sexual act is to the normal person. For the fetishist has displaced his desire from an area in which it can be fulfilled to an area in which it cannot. It has been moved from a sensation to an idea; and since sexuality, although enormously dependent upon ideas, is ultimately only fulfilled through a sensation, people suffering from this deviation are prevented from ever finding the same degree of satisfaction which their more fortunate brethren obtain so much more easily.

All degrees of fetishism exist, from the true deviation, in which the fetish is substituted for the person and simply used for masturbation, to the much commoner condition in which the fetish serves simply as a means by which the man can be sure that his desire will be fully aroused and that he will be potent enough to fulfil it. There are many men with mild degrees of fetishism who, during intercourse, have recourse to phantasies in which the fetish plays some part. This is especially so when they are fatigued, or when, for some reason, intercourse is not proving wholly satisfactory. Since those who suffer from fetishistic compulsions usually have an abnormal degree of sexual guilt, it is often difficult for them to admit their particular preference to their partner; or, if they can bring themselves to do so, they do it in such a way that the girl also regards their request for her to wear a particular scent or a particular garment as abnormal. In general, since women do not share the male's interest in fetishes, they are apt to be unsympathetic to male demands that they should wear some particular garment, feeling that the man loves a thing rather than themselves. But the woman who is experienced in coquetry, and who understands the complexities of the male psyche, will come to realize that such demands are but *rites d'entrée* – ways of arousing the man so that he may love her better, means rather than ends in themselves – and therefore no reflection upon her own attractiveness.

Men who, for the reasons given above, are unable to satisfy their proclivities at home may turn elsewhere. *The Ladies' Directory*, a pamphlet giving the descriptions and telephone numbers of prostitutes which was the subject of a recent prosecution, was full of advertisements in which Miss X drew attention not only to her physical charms but also to her willingness to 'model rainwear' or wear any garment which her clients might ask for. There is no doubt that, in an age when partners for orthodox sexual activities are not difficult to find, it is largely the readiness of prostitutes to cater for various forms of deviation which keeps them in business.

Fetishism has a compulsive quality; and, indeed, the phantasy which accompanies the fetish may be compared with an obsessional thought. Like the latter, it is not deliberately willed, it is often alien to the person's conscious intention, and the man who suffers from it frequently wants to be rid of it. Many fetishists show other features of the obsessional character: rigidity, meticulousness, a fear of dirt, and a tendency to hoard. Naturally enough, one of the things which may be hoarded is the fetish; and there are cases reported of people who make enormous collections of shoes, pigtails, or other fetish objects. The connexion between this and normal 'collecting' is interesting, and analysis might probably reveal that many collections of stamps, matchboxes, wine-labels, and other objects which are not commonly fetishes yet had a sexual significance at an unconscious level.

Occasionally the desire for the fetish provokes stealing, and some of the more bizarre thefts, such as those of women's underclothes from washing-lines are the work of fetishists pursuing their aberration. In general, however, fetishists are timid people who live withdrawn lives and do no harm to anyone else; and, since every man harbours within himself embryonic forms of fetishism, it is to be hoped that widening understanding may breed compassion for this common sexual deviation.

6

Transvestism

In Buñuel's film *Viridiana* we are shown a sequence in which a bearded, elderly widower goes to the chest in which he has kept his wife's clothes since her death on their wedding-day many years before. He attempts to dress himself in some of them, but is interrupted before he can do so. It is obvious that he is trying to recreate the image of his bride, and that he is using her clothes to lend this image some semblance of reality. In the last chapter we saw how the fetishist may, partially or completely, substitute his fetish for a woman; and we attributed his compulsion to do this to his failure to make a fully satisfying relationship with a woman in reality, because of the persistence within him from childhood of fears of the opposite sex. The transvestite, who suffers from similar fears, goes one step further, and finds sexual arousal and release by himself dressing in the garments which, for him, have come to represent femininity. These are generally the same clothes referred to in the last chapter as likely to become fetishes. The commonest transvestite practice is for a man to dress himself in such clothes and then masturbate, often while looking at himself in a mirror. Pleasure is obtained from the sensuous feel of the feminine garments, which are often described as giving the same tender, caressing sensation which is more usually obtained from the touch of a woman's body.

Some men, insufficiently confident in their masculinity to enjoy such sartorial display as is permitted to the male in our society, experience an exhibitionistic pleasure when dressed as women. Still others, sado-masochistically inclined, find pleasure in the tightness and restriction which they impose on themselves by wearing feminine clothes which involve these discomforts. Usually there is an attempt to create a phantasy woman of extreme seductiveness, a courtesan who will arouse the maximum desire. Such a phantasy figure exists in the minds of all men – the woman who is nothing but mistress, who makes no demands, and who exists solely that she may please her lover. As an example of transvestism, we may quote the case of a man, who although happily married and having regular, though rather infrequent sexual relations with his wife, felt compelled to dress in her clothes about once a week. This activity made him intensely excited, and gave him a feeling of great potency. Instead of finding himself unmanned by being dressed as a woman, as one might imagine would be likely, he actually experienced an increase of self-confidence, and felt more of a man than when he was dressed in his ordinary clothes.

At one level, such a man is trying to create an imaginary woman, just as the widower in *Viridiana* is trying to recapture his lost wife. By dressing in feminine clothes and acting the role himself he can conjure up whatever kind of woman he likes. She can be tender or passionate; kind or cruel; dominant or yielding. She will wear exactly what he wants her to wear, and behave precisely as he desires without his being faced with the situation of having to impose his will upon a real person at all. In the shadow-play before the looking-glass he can himself take on the part which he has always hoped a girl will act for him, but which he has never succeeded in getting anyone to play because of his own inhibitions and fears in any sexual situation with a real woman.

At a deeper level, the transvestite is actually identifying himself with a woman. The fetishist has substituted a thing for a person, but is still emotionally involved with an object which is not himself. The transvestite is also involved with the clothes he assumes, and may be said to be having sexual relations with them instead of with a person: but, in addition, the transvestite himself becomes in phantasy the woman with whom, in reality, he has failed to make an adequately close relationship.

In Chapter 3 we referred to the process of identification as a necessary and valuable part of growing-up; and pointed out that, in the ordinary family, the developing child learned to play the sexual role expected of it by modelling itself upon the parent of the same sex. In at least some cases of transvestism, this process has gone astray, and the developing boy has, unconsciously, identified himself more with the mother than with the father. In the case referred to above, the subject's father was a weak man who played little part in family life and who habitually deferred to his wife. It was the mother of the family who 'wore the trousers'. It was the mother, therefore, who represented to her son the qualities of forcefulness, decisiveness, and dominance which generally pertain to the father in more happily constituted families; and by identifying himself with her the son was actually being more 'masculine' than if he had modelled himself upon his inadequate father. It is thus possible to understand how it is that a man can, paradoxically, feel himself to be more of a man when he is dressed as a woman.

That this kind of explanation is insufficient to account for transvestism is obvious. For there are many families in which the mother is the dominant figure, but in which the sons do not become transvestites. We do not know all the factors which together combine so that a man is compelled to choose this particular solution to his sexual problems. That the matter is complicated may be inferred from the remarks that follow. The psychoanalytic interpretation of transvestism runs as follows. *The homosexual man replaces his love for his mother by an identification with her: the fetishist refuses to acknowledge that a woman has no penis. The male transvestite assumes both attitudes simultaneously. He fantasies that the woman possesses a penis, and thus overcomes his castration anxiety, and identifies himself with this phallic woman.*

This formula does less than justice to the compensatory, play-acting aspect of transvestite behaviour, which has been referred to above. There is no doubt that the transvestite is trying to make up for what is missing in his actual relations with women by imagining a seductive courtesan who will arouse in him a strong

erotic response. But many men do this without having recourse
to cross-dressing, although they may stimulate their imagination
with erotic pictures and in other ways. The transvestite is indeed
identifying himself with a phallic woman, as the psychoanalysts
affirm, and his behaviour requires further explanation.

In the example given above the mother was a dominant, forceful, rather masculine woman, who might well be regarded as
'phallic'. But it may not be necessary for a boy to have a mother
of this kind for him to make this type of identification. In one
sense, and at a very primitive level, all mothers are phallic.
Everyone is familiar with the figure of the witch, with her pointed
hat and broomstick; and her counterparts can be found all over
the world in various guises. Masculine symbols are constantly
found in association with mother goddesses, especially those with
a frightening witch-like aspect. Hecate, for example, is associated
with the key, the whip, the dagger, and the torch. To the small
child, the mother can be a terrifying figure, as well as the person
to whom he clings; and these various representations of women
as threatening and powerful can be interpreted as demonstrating
this. That mothers can be a threat to their children hardly needs
proof. Most people will know from their own experience of
cases in which a mother has possessively clung to a son, destroy-
ing his independence, blackmailing him into staying with her,
preventing his marriage. Such mothers are indeed witches, who
have stolen their son's masculinity. In the *Malleus Maleficarum*,
that terrible medieval manual of the witch-hunter, witches are
reputed to steal men's penises, as well as rendering them impotent
in other ways.

For a man to identify himself with a woman may, therefore, be
a process in which he does not deprive himself of masculinity, as
symbolized by the penis, but rather gains possession of it; since
the woman with whom he identifies himself can be this primitive
type of powerful mother-figure, who is masculine as well as
feminine.

For such an identification to occur it is necessary to postulate
an emotional immaturity of a rather profound kind. A boy, in the
course of normal development, has to separate himself from his

mother in order to achieve masculine independence. It argues a fairly complete failure to do this if he identifies with her in this way, for this manoeuvre implies clinging to her as well as childishly regarding her as powerful. Such an identification also betokens a failure to relate emotionally to any person other than the mother. The transvestite whose case was quoted above was happily married, but he was unable to be fully in love with his wife owing to the persistence of the emotional tie with his mother.

It is generally assumed by those who are not familiar with this deviation that transvestism is a form of homosexuality, and statements to this effect can even be found in textbooks of psychiatry. But, as Kinsey points out, there is really nothing to support this: *Transvestism and homosexuality are totally independent phenomena, and it is only a small portion of the transvestites who are homosexual in their physical relationships.*

It is true that some homosexuals occasionally assume female clothes, usually at 'drag' parties, or when soliciting as prostitutes; but the clothes are worn for their effect upon others rather than as a means of obtaining satisfaction for the man himself. Transvestites are essentially people who are uncertain of their masculinity and consequently diffident in their sexual approaches to women. But they show no conscious sexual interest in men, and their identification with women and their interest in all that appertains to femininity demonstrates how strongly the tide of their libido flows in a heterosexual direction.

There are a number of historical examples of men who have spent much of their lives dressed as women, of whom the best-known are the Abbé de Choisy and the Chevalier d'Eon de Beaumont. Transvestism is sometimes known as Eonism; a term derived from the name of the latter, who was an eighteenth-century French diplomat. There are also examples of women who have habitually dressed as males; but the significance of transvestism in the female is different from that in the male, as will be explained below.

That mythical creature the 'normal' man may find some difficulty in understanding or sympathizing with transvestite behaviour, since he may not easily be able to detect any such tendency in himself. However, the desire to dress as the opposite sex is widely catered for vicariously in public entertainment. There are nearly always night clubs to be found in any big city which advertise a transvestite entertainer as one of their main attractions, and the traditional Christmas pantomime inevitably contains a 'dame' who is a man as well as a 'principal boy' who is a girl. Some transvestites are able to make their deviation into a way of earning a living by appearing as female impersonators.

It is clear that, although the image of the phallic woman may be deeply buried in the mists of infantile experience, most men are capable of the kind of imaginative sympathy with others which is commonly and perhaps significantly referred to as putting oneself in another person's shoes, and are thus capable of identifying themselves with the opposite sex to some extent. Indeed, if this was not so, civilization would hardly be possible. It is only when we recognize other people, whether male or female, as being like ourselves, and can therefore imagine that they think and feel as we do, that we treat them humanely. This capacity for imaginative sympathy, or empathy, as it is often called, is a less primitive form of identification than that which obtains in the parent-child relationship, but it is none the less important. Havelock Ellis attributed transvestism entirely to an exaggeration of the normal tendency to identify oneself with a beloved person. This explanation is obviously insufficient, but certainly plays some part in many cases of this deviation.

When, in *Free Fall*, William Golding describes a lad's infatuation, he beautifully conveys the perfectly normal desire to know what it is to *be* the person with whom one is in love.

'Beatrice.'
'Mm?'
'What is it like to be you?'
A sensible question; and asked out of my admiration for Evie and Ma, out of my adolescent fantasies, out of my painful obsession with discovery and identification. An impossible question.
'Just ordinary.'
What is it like to hold the centre of someone's universe, to be soft

and fair and sweet, to be neat and clean by nature, to be desired to distraction, to live under this hair, behind these huge, unutterable eyes, to feel the lift of these guarded twins, the valley, the plunge down to the tiny waist, to be vulnerable and invulnerable? What is it like in the bath and the lavatory and walking the pavement with shorter steps and high heels; what is it like to know your body breathes this faint perfume which makes my heart burst and my senses swim?

All human relationships of a deep kind are a blend between identity and difference. If a woman finds a man incomprehensible, or a man regards a woman as entirely mysterious, neither is likely to achieve much human understanding of the other, although they may be able to make a satisfactory sexual relation on the physical plane alone. More romantic lovers habitually feel that they are the same as each other, and delightedly recognize similarities of taste, belief, and outlook. Nevertheless, if they were exactly the same, their love would not be love in the full sense, quite apart from the necessary physical difference; for love depends on the ability of the partner to complete what is lacking in oneself, and hence upon the differences from oneself which the partner shows. Love which is based upon a recognition of identity alone is incomplete – a subject to which we shall return when discussing homosexuality. But the wish to *be* the other person, and hence to be the opposite sex to some degree is a component part of everyone's nature; and the greatest novelists have generally been distinguished by an unusual capacity for identifying themselves with either sex.

While transvestism is generally practised as a masturbatory ritual in the way described above by men who only wish to dress as women during periods of erotic excitement, there do exist others who would prefer permanently to assume a feminine identity. Such men occasionally seek medical advice in the hope that some surgeon may, by operation, 'change their sex'.

There are rare and unfortunate individuals who are born with such anatomical abnormalities of the sexual organs that their sex is indeterminate. Occasionally, such hermaphrodites are reared as one sex, but decide in adult life to change to the other; and a surgeon may, in some instances, perform an operation designed to emphasize the characteristics of the sex decided upon, while removing traces of that discarded. This is very far from changing the sex of an individual with normal organs, and such an operation is of course impossible.

Those who demand it are generally men who have given up all hope of competing with other males on anything approaching equal terms. They hope that, by submitting to castration and adopting the dress and occupation of females, they will solve their emotional problems. But the hard facts of anatomy and physiology preclude a surgical solution; and, although some men find a certain relief in dressing permanently as women and abandoning the struggle to be masculine, they are not thereby enabled to become feminine in anything but superficialities.

Such people are much more deeply disturbed in mind than the transvestite who compulsively dresses in female clothes to obtain sexual satisfaction. The phantasy of becoming the opposite sex is a common initial symptom of that profound disorder we call schizophrenia; and those who express the delusion that such a change is actually occurring are invariably psychotic. Although the assertion of change of sex by the incipient schizophrenic is not to be taken literally, it nevertheless expresses a figurative truth. In schizophrenia, the patient's ego, the 'I' with which he normally identifies himself, is overwhelmed, so that he is no longer able to exercise conscious control, and is at the mercy of phantasy and unconscious contents. The idea that a change of sex is occurring is one way of expressing this loss of ego-control. Normally, a person identifies the conscious ego with his own sex. In an earlier chapter the importance of being able to identify oneself with one's own sex was discussed. But the conscious ego is not the whole of our personality. If it were, we should not be able to feel empathy with, or to identify with, members of the opposite sex. The inner, emotional, and partially unconscious aspect of our personality has the character of the opposite sex – a fact recognized by Jung when he called the masculine side of a woman the animus, and the feminine side of a man the anima. When a man and a woman are happily united sexually, this opposite aspect of themselves is not obvious; for each experiences it in the other person. But men separated from women by circumstances or by fear tend to be over-emotional in what could be called a feminine way; whilst women separated from men often show a kind of pseudo-masculinity in being domineering or dogmatic.

In seeking to understand transvestism, we must recognize that we are all partially bisexual. This is true even anatomically; for every man has rudimentary female organs, and every woman has certain masculine characteristics. The female clitoris, for example, is simply a tiny penis. It is composed of the same kind of tissue as the male organ, and becomes congested with blood during sexual excitement in a comparable manner. In male anatomy, the most obvious feminine feature is the breast, an organ which is generally rudimentary in men, but which can be made to expand to female proportions by the administration of suitable hormones. There are other less obvious examples of this admixture. Perhaps if we did not possess some of the features of the other sex we should be less able than we are to understand and come to terms with our opposites.

Transvestism, like fetishism, is a sexual deviation of the male. Women often assume masculine dress, and identify themselves to some extent with men, a condition which will be further discussed in Chapter 7. But female cross-dressing is seldom if ever compulsive, and is not undertaken for the immediate purpose of erotic satisfaction. Women may, and often do want to be men, but they do not use male clothes as a substitute for the man himself.

It is partly because transvestism has a different significance in the two sexes that, in our culture, women dressed in masculine clothes are more readily accepted than men dressed in feminine clothes. It is sometimes assumed that male transvestism is illegal, but this is not the case. A man may dress as he pleases, provided that he does not offend against public decency by exposing his genitals. But, since it is not generally realized that the majority of transvestite males are heterosexual, a man who dresses publicly as a woman may be assumed by the police to be importuning or soliciting for immoral purposes. The different attitude of society towards transvestism in the two sexes is part of the same prejudice which ignores homosexuality in the female whilst severely penalizing the same deviation in the male.

7

Female Homosexuality

The term homosexual is derived from the Greek prefix *homo*, meaning 'the same as', and not, as many people suppose, from the Latin word for man. It is, therefore, an appropriate word to describe erotic love between two persons of the same sex, whether they be male or female. The words 'lesbian' and 'sapphic' are also sometimes used of sexual relationships between women, referring to the fact that the Greek poetess Sappho, who lived on the island of Lesbos, was herself homosexual.

Homosexual relationships between women are statistically less common than those between men. Nevertheless, when Kinsey investigated the frequency with which women recognized their own erotic responses to other women, he discovered that, by the age of thirty, twenty-five per cent of his large sample had been aware of such feelings in themselves, and, by the age of forty, nineteen per cent had had some physical contact with a female which was intended to be sexual by one or other of the pair. Since female homosexuality is proscribed by law in only a few countries, and seldom prosecuted in those countries where it is condemned, it tends to excite less comment than male homosexuality; and there are very few cases recorded of women soliciting homosexually or seducing minors. As with other forms of sexual activity, it appears that compulsive, repetitive behaviour is generally confined to men; and that women, whether they be homosexual or heterosexual, are not so violently driven by their sexual impulses that they cannot generally postpone their need for satisfaction. This characteristic of women's sexual life as compared with that of men is in line with a general tendency towards extensity rather than intensity. For example, women often seem able to sustain a mild effort over a long period better than men, whereas men are more capable of short, intense bursts of activity which they intersperse with periods of complete inactivity which are seldom allowed to women.

On account of society's attitude, homosexual attachments between women tend to be less conspicuous and less guilt-ridden than those between men. Moreover, whereas male homosexuality is almost invariably expressed by mutual masturbation and other physical practices, feminine homosexuality is often confined to the psychological level, with perhaps no physical manifestations at all beyond the tender embraces which our society generally accepts as being a natural accompaniment of friendship between women.

People who think of sexuality as an isolated thing, without realizing that it runs like a scarlet thread intimately interwoven into the pattern of all our affections, may be shocked when the psychiatrist discerns homosexuality in all attachments between women living together. But it is in truth an artificiality to separate sex and affection; and the fact that there is a physical element in all emotional relationships, whether recognized or not, and whether acted upon or not, is surely nothing about which to be alarmed or of which to be ashamed. We may dichotomize ourselves into mind and body; but, especially in our affections, this division cannot be maintained.

In Great Britain there has, for a number of years, been a superfluity of females; so that many women who would like to do so fail to get married. It may be argued that these women are likely to be those who are in some way inhibited sexually, and who therefore might not get married even if there were plenty of men to go round; and of course this is bound to be true of a certain proportion. Nevertheless, there are a number of women who could have made a happy marriage, but who do not do so; and such people are left with a need for human companionship which leads them to set up house with another woman rather than remain on their own. The emotional links which spring up between people who share their lives together often become strong; for which of us, unless we are notably eccentric, can exist entirely alone? It is not surprising that a relationship which may be entered upon for companionship often develops sexual concomitants.

Both women and men share with many species of animal the capacity to find sexual satisfaction with their own sex when the opposite sex is unavailable; which is partly why homosexuality is especially prevalent in schools, religious communities, and other groups from which the opposite sex is excluded. The comparative shortage of men in a society which does not permit polygamy may account, therefore, for a proportion of the emotional attachments between women which are so common amongst us, but it is far from being the whole explanation.

What causes a woman who has a reasonable opportunity of mixing with the opposite sex to cling persistently to her own, and reject the chance of marriage and children? Although much has been written on this subject, it is still impossible to give a clear-cut answer, for the adoption of a homosexual solution is the outcome of a mixture of many psychopathological factors which interact with one another in a complicated way. What follows is a description and discussion of some of these factors.

To many women, the idea of a sexual contact, or even of a strongly emotional relationship with one of their own number, appears distasteful. Yet, if they look back to childhood and the beginnings of adolescence, they will probably recall several girls or women who were important to them in an irrational, emotional way which can only be compared with falling in love, since it is actually one form of this experience. Such attachments are an important part of growing-up, for they enable the developing girl to become aware of new aspects of her own feminine personality. All of us, male or female, tend to be fascinated by, and to fall in love with, people who represent some aspect of ourselves which is not finding expression in actual life. It is easy to see this in extreme examples, for instance, the fascination of the crudest sensuality for the one-sided intellectual, exemplified by the professor who becomes infatuated with the night-club singer in

The Blue Angel; or, in homosexual terms, the passion of the scholar-poet for the athlete as illustrated by A. E. Housman. In such cases, the person who is in love appears to be enthralled by his opposite. But since all of us contain in varying proportion all the elements which go to make up that bundle of complex contradictions, a human being, the opposites by which we are attracted may also be said to be undeveloped parts of ourselves; aspects of our own human nature which have been either repressed or neglected. This concept, to which we shall return, is valuable in understanding any powerful attraction between human beings; but it is especially applicable to homosexual infatuations.

When a girl comes back from school full of enthusiasm for a new 'special friend', or extolling the virtues of a particular teacher, parents recognize that such attractions, which are usually ephemeral, are a normal part of growing-up. To label these 'crushes' homosexual may offend those to whom this adjective is an abusive rather than a descriptive term; but to others, more open-minded, an understanding of the crush and a recollection of their own experience of it may open the door to a more sympathetic understanding of those who have remained arrested at this stage of their emotional development.

We have already spoken of the developing child's need for models with whom to identify as he or she prepares to take on the adult sexual role expected by society. Ordinarily, the principal female model will be the mother; and it is upon her attitude to her own femininity that her daughters will base their ideas of what it is to be a woman. A fortunate girl will have a mother who is happily in love with her father, and who also enjoys her maternal function, and who thus conveys, from the child's earliest days, that to be a woman who is loved by a man and who has children by him is the first and most important aim of feminine existence. But, even the most serenely feminine of mothers cannot be so complete a person that she is able to exemplify and evoke every potentiality which her daughters may contain within them. For their full development they need to be exposed to many influences – to those of teachers, of friends, and of other members of the family. A varying number of these people may, for a time, assume an especial importance in the girl's eyes. The emotion which she feels can range from simple admiration and liking to a passionate adoration which entirely absorbs her. In the latter case, the girl generally feels at first that the object of her affections is greatly superior to herself, and that she cannot possibly aspire to equality with her. Very often, the qualities which she so much admires in the older person are more imagined than real; and many a young teacher, aware of her own deficiencies, must be astonished to find that a pupil attributes to her the wisdom of the ages and the beauty of Cleopatra. This phenomenon is one example of the psychological mechanism we call projection. The girl projects upon the woman an image which actually springs from within herself; an image of an idealized woman possessing all the virtues, but displaying none of the deficiencies which inevitably accompany those virtues in an actual human being.

This ideal image represents what the girl would like to be herself, and so she proceeds to model herself upon the woman she so much admires. In more technical terms, one can say that projection is followed by an attempt at identification; and the girl can often be seen to adopt the manner, style of dress, and interests of the older woman, only to drop them in favour of those of another person when her first enthusiasm has died down.

This process of projection followed by identification is part of the normal pattern of growing-up. It is an attempt, unconsciously directed, of the immature to discover and to realize their own identities as members of their own sex; a reaching-out towards adult status. It can, therefore, be seen to operate in every one of us. Those who deny that they have ever had an emotional feeling towards one of their own sex have generally forgotten the heroes or heroines of their pre-adolescent youth.

In the normal course of events, this process of self-discovery ends by the girl becoming reasonably confident in herself as a desirable woman and a potentially adequate mother. When once this stage is achieved, she will no longer see other women as particularly wonderful or superior to herself, in accordance with the general principle that we most admire that which we do not ourselves possess or feel capable of achieving. A normally confident woman is competitive with other women; but she does not adore femininity in others, since she herself has it as part of her own nature. By being able to identify herself with an adult woman, she automatically withdraws the projection which, in earlier years, lent older women a kind of glamour for her.

Many girls, however, fail to take this step, and so remain in a state of mind where they believe themselves to be deficient as feminine beings. This sense of sexual inferiority has two consequences. First, it results in the girl turning away from attempts at heterosexual contacts, since she does not believe that men will find her desirable, even if she herself is conscious of any feeling towards them. Secondly, she remains in the pre-adolescent condition of retaining an emotional interest in her own sex, in the way described above. This varies in intensity from a mild admiration for other women to a compulsive, intensely emotional drive to find a feminine partner which may be uncontrollable.

Although every girl probably experiences some attraction towards her own sex in the course of her development, this phenomenon is particularly marked in instances where the girl's relationship with her mother has been defective. If, for any of a large variety of reasons, this vital link has proved inadequate, two main consequences may follow which interact and reinforce one another. Firstly, the daughter will not develop that inner sense of security for which a good relationship with the mother in early years is a prerequisite. Secondly, it will be more difficult for the daughter to discover her own identity as a woman if her mother has proved to be a poor model of femininity with which to identify.

Women who are predominantly homosexual usually show evidence of a deep sense of insecurity in general, as well as a failure to realize their own femininity. This is why so many homosexual attachments are characterized by an even stronger element of dependency than is usually found in heterosexual couples. For the homosexual woman is generally looking for a mother as well as for a sexual partner: and, in many instances, the mutual dependence of the couple upon each other is more important than the sexual satisfaction which each may obtain from the other. Indeed, the intense jealousy which often springs up if one partner becomes involved with an outside companion seems more like the rivalry of children competing for a parent's attention than the result of damaged adult sexual pride.

In cases where a girl has been grossly deprived of maternal love, perhaps because of the illness or early death of her mother, the search for a mother substitute may be compulsive. In one such instance, a woman was so driven by her need to compensate for the lack of her own mother that she attached herself to a whole series of older women, who, one after the other, proved inadequate to her needs. A severely deprived person will tend in adult life to make emotional demands upon others which they cannot fulfil, since she is asking for the love and attention which a child of three or less may justifiably demand from its mother, but which cannot generally be given by one adult to another. This particular woman needed the kind of mothering which is only given to small babies. She needed to feel that, for a time, her requirements were paramount, so that, if she wanted attention from her mother-substitute, the latter should at once abandon every other pursuit and rush to her side. Moreover, she was unable to tolerate any kind of attention being given to anyone else, and would fly into violent rages in which she attacked the mother-substitute physically if she believed that her place was being usurped by another. It was scarcely surprising, but nonetheless tragic, that none of the women to whom she became attached could ultimately put up with her demands, or fulfil her need to be totally dependent. It is very difficult to learn that in life it often pays to be least importunate about what one most desires.

This is an extreme example; but it illustrates a pattern which can be detected in less degree in many lesbian relationships which are predominantly and basically mother–daughter relationships. As we have pointed out, the 'daughter' of the two is seeking two things: a mother upon whom to depend; and a feminine model with whom to identify, as in the adolescent crush; and these two elements may be blended in varying proportions. What of the other member of the pair, the 'mother'? In many examples of homosexual couples it is fairly obvious that one, if not both, of the pair is gaining considerable satisfaction for her maternal instinct. The majority of women want to have someone to cherish and care for, and, if they fail to have children, seek a substitute to compensate for this lack. It is natural enough that a childless woman should lavish maternal affection upon another who is generally young for her age and in need of emotional support.

Such a relationship can only be partially satisfactory. It is hardly possible for a woman to play the part of a mother towards another person who is not in reality her child without some intermittent resentment of the demands which are made upon her; for she is unlikely to be as profoundly tolerant as are the majority of mothers towards children whom they have actually borne. Moreover, that part of her own nature which requires the support which a man might give her will remain unfulfilled. Almost inevitably, she will at times try to obtain from her partner exactly what the latter is unable to grant her; the love of an adult who can give as well as receive. Many such relationships, therefore, are marred by hostilities and tensions in which one or both partners feel that the other is giving less than she is receiving.

In many homosexual partnerships, it is obvious that one of the couple plays a dominant role which is more masculine than maternal. Everyone is familiar with the conventional picture of the lesbian who adopts a pseudo-masculine way of dressing and talking, and who appears to despise anything feminine in herself as weakness. Thirty years ago England seemed peculiarly apt at producing a stalwart breed of commanding women clad in collars and ties, tweeds and boots, striding manfully through life with hair cut short and faces innocent of cosmetics. Increasing psychological sophistication has diminished the numbers of those who display their adoption of the masculine role so blatantly;

but there are many women who are more or less identified with the male who do not show this in so obvious a way.

The reasons for such an identification vary. It has long been recognized by analysts of different schools that most girls have at some stage in their development an envy of the male. Alfred Adler's phrase 'masculine protest', the Freudian 'penis envy', and Jung's concept of the animus-ridden woman each refer to a complex of emotions, shared by all women to some extent, in which resentment of so-called male superiority is intermingled with aggressive 'masculine' attitudes and a tendency to denigrate the ways of men. One of the most fascinating and perplexing aspects of feminine behaviour is that women without men, or women whose emotional contact with men is deficient, tend both to express contempt for men and yet also to behave in some ways like the sex they affect to despise. Such behaviour can generally be traced back to childhood, for very many girls go through a stage of development in which they openly avow their desire to be boys, want to wear masculine clothes, and long to take part in the games and activities which tradition assigns to the boy rather than to the girl. In the eyes of the child, boys are more power-ful, more independent, and more adventurous. Since every normal child wishes to grow up and be free of the trammels of adult authority, it is natural enough that both boys and girls should reach out towards the power that they feel to be lacking in them-selves and that appears to belong predominantly to the male. It is generally more pathological for a boy to wish to be a girl than for a girl to want to be a boy; and by far the majority of girls who, at eight or nine, play the cowboy become fully heterosexual in later life. There is, therefore, no reason for parents to be alarmed if their daughter goes through a stage of being a tomboy. In certain instances, however, this male identification is not abandoned. One girl, who in adult life was predominantly homosexual, had a father who was a violent and brutal man, and who frequently beat her. Very early she contracted so intense a hatred for him that she passionately wished to be a boy in order that, when she grew up, she would be strong enough to retaliate, a mechanism described by psychoanalysts as 'identification with the aggressor'.

Moreover, she was conditioned to feel that to be feminine was to be inferior, for her father had wanted a son rather than a daughter, and it was partly on this account that he so maltreated her. She felt uncomfortable in feminine clothes, and eschewed all the normal devices by which women make themselves more enticing; for her mother had not succeeded either in protecting her from her father or in making the feminine role seem in any way attractive to her. She repudiated any attempt to make contact with men, since the picture of the male with which her father had presented her was so repulsive; but her need for affection and sexual satisfaction drove her to seek love from other women who might temporarily assuage, although they could not cure, her angry isolation.

Such a girl is an example of the fact that homosexual behaviour is generally the product of the interaction of many psychological factors. Often both parents are themselves inadequate, as in this instance, in which neither was able to function as either a loving spouse or as a loving parent. Some writers suppose that there is an inherited, constitutional factor or some disturbance of the endocrine glands which accounts for feminine homosexuality; but there is little evidence to support this. On the other hand, whilst we may accept the fact that every woman is capable of homosexual responses, it is difficult to agree with Kinsey that accidental contacts and simple conditioning are enough to account for a woman choosing a way of life which must leave a good deal of her nature unsatisfied. This is not to deny that between two women the sexual relation itself may be physically satisfying. Although some women may feel a sense of disappointment in that another woman is unable to play the masculine role by actively penetrating them, many appear to achieve full orgasm by mutual masturbation. The penis is not so essential to feminine pleasure as men would like to believe.

Homosexual relationships between women tend to be more persistent and perhaps more satisfying than their male equivalents. Nevertheless, this solution is always *faute de mieux*, and those lesbians who protest that, for them, this kind of relationship is better than any possible intimacy with a man do not know what they are really missing. There is no doubt that for women who, for whatever reason, have been unable to get married, a homosexual partnership may be a happier way of life than a frustrated loneliness; but this is not to say that it can ever be fully satisfying.

8   Male Homosexuality

Male homosexuality differs from female homosexuality in several respects, notably in the fact that it has been the subject of more detailed study. The belief that this common sexual deviation is an inherited constitutional abnormality is affirmed by many; but evidence for this is so far unconvincing. The present state of our knowledge is that, while there may be some congenital predisposition to develop homosexually, the genetic basis for this is uncertain; and there is certainly no reason to suppose that homosexuality is determined by a specific gene as in the case of familial diseases like Huntington's chorea. It has recently been demonstrated that male homosexuals tend to be born of elderly mothers, and to arrive later in the family than their brothers and sisters. This has been taken to indicate that a chromosomal abnormality may be responsible for their deviation, since it is known that such abnormalities are more frequently found in the offspring of elderly mothers. However, the facts are also susceptible of a purely psychological explanation, since the late arrivals in a family often mature more slowly than the elder children, and the relation between a youngest son and an ageing mother is sometimes one of particular emotional intensity. Whether or not genetic factors play a part, there is a great deal to suggest that the male homosexual is made, not born; and that his sexual preference in adult life is determined by the emotional influences to which he has been exposed in early childhood.

In the last chapter we discussed how it was that a girl could remain in an immature stage of development in which her emotional interest was directed towards her own sex. It was suggested that a number of different psychopathological factors might combine to produce the result of a predominantly homosexual orientation in adult life, and some of these factors were outlined. Many of the same factors can be found to operate in male homosexuality, although there are differences in behaviour of male homosexuals as compared with their lesbian counterparts.

So much has recently been written upon the topic of male homosexuality that it is impossible to discuss the condition fully within the confines of a single chapter or even a single book. What follows, therefore, is not an attempt to compete with the excellent studies of D. J. West and others, but a brief and tentative statement of the author's point of view on a complex problem in which unsupported assertions still outnumber facts derived from adequate research.

There can be no possible doubt that homosexual behaviour is potential within every man. Kinsey discovered that no less than thirty-seven per cent of males have had some homosexual experience; and anthropological data from societies other than our own show that, in more tolerant cultures, one hundred per cent of males engage in homosexual as well as heterosexual activity. In schools, in prisons, and in the forces, homosexuality is so common that it may seem pedantic to call it abnormal; and yet there is much to suggest that those males who remain exclusively homosexual are actually immature in the same kind of way as their female counterparts.

Many homosexual males will themselves deny this. Some flaunt their sexual preference, alleging that they belong to a select group which is especially distinguished for sensitivity and creative ability; others conceal their tastes and conform as closely as possible to the conventional image of the ordinary male. A few unusually well-balanced homosexuals neither deny nor advertise the tendency of their emotions, and appear to accept their own nature philosophically. All, however, have a vested interest in affirming that their condition is an inborn abnormality rather than the result of circumstances; for any other explanation is bound to imply a criticism either of themselves or of their families, and usually of both.

If the ability to have fully satisfying relations with the opposite sex is accepted as one criterion of emotional maturity, as suggested in the opening chapters of this book, it follows that to be homosexual is to be immature: and, however one may argue that such a condition is a result of circumstances outside the control of the individual, a failure to surmount those circumstances is implied, which reflects upon the person concerned in a way in which a purely genetic explanation does not. If our faults can be attributed to our stars or to our chromosomes, we do not feel as responsible for them as we do for those which can be attributed to the errors of our parents, and to our own difficulties in overcoming those errors. For we find it hard to believe that such childhood influences can damage us irrevocably, and tend to imagine that we ought to be able, by force of will, to direct the course of our own lives, even when our upbringing may have been such as to render this impossible. Nevertheless, research into the family background of male homosexuals has already yielded results which tend to show that certain specific family patterns are particularly likely to produce a homosexual son.

Of these patterns, by far the commonest is one in which the father is detached from, and either shows little affection for, or is actually hostile to the son in question; combined with a mother who is extremely intimate and over-emotional. This particular combination is likely to produce homosexuality for the following reasons. The developing boy requires a male model with whom to identify if he is to discover his own masculinity. As we stated in Chapter 3, the father is the male with whom the boy will generally identify himself most closely in the first instance; and this process is made easier if the attitude of father to son is one of affectionate encouragement. But many fathers are indifferent to, or actually jealous of their sons; and in such instances, the son may turn away from his father and strive to be as unlike him as possible. Fear of a hostile father may also have the effect of making the son timid and unable to assert himself physically or mentally. An excessive fear of physical injury is more commonly found in male homosexuals than in heterosexuals.

It is when such a negative relation to the father is accompanied by a particularly intimate relation with the mother that homosexuality is most apt to result. It has been discovered that, in many instances, the son who becomes homosexual is his mother's confidant and favourite. This close emotional tie, which is often accompanied by excessive physical caressing, is likely to awaken a premature eroticism in the son, whilst at the same time denying it fulfilment. One characteristic feature of the erotic behaviour of homosexuals is that, compared with that of heterosexuals, it tends to begin at an earlier age.

The significance of the incest taboo has been discussed in a previous chapter. Here, it is sufficient to point out that a mother who overwhelms her son with this false kind of affection, or who tries to make him into a substitute for an unsatisfactory husband, is likely to deter him from attempting any relationship with other women. For she will implant within him the picture of woman as a dangerous seductress who will deprive him of his masculinity rather than encourage its expression, and in later life he will be likely to view all women in this light, whenever a specifically erotic relation with one is in question. The danger of the erotic advance from mother to son lies in the fact that the son, while still a child, cannot imagine being in the dominant role *vis-à-vis* his mother. His relation to her is essentially one of dependency, a condition which is incompatible with the proper expression of male sexuality. It can often be shown that in adult life, male homosexuals get on excellently with women; but this is so only so long as no erotic element enters into the relationship to make it dangerous. For the homosexual, women are safe only so long as they are platonic companions. Any suggestion that they might be mistresses renders them alarming.

For every boy, the relationship to the mother is a threat as well as a necessary aspect of childhood security. In the beginning, he needs her loving protection; but, as he gets older, he must emancipate himself, or else he remains tied to her apron strings, a castrated boy who is never able to realize his full masculine potential. This is why, in myth and legend, women are so often portrayed as witches or enchantresses, whose feminine power is a threat to the hero. The homosexual's fear of women springs from his difficulty in breaking clear of his mother. For him, to become emotionally involved with a woman is to retreat once more into arms which may be loving but which form a prison from which he has in any case only partially escaped. It is an exaggeration of a fear which is present in every man in minor degree: for which of us can claim to have entirely discarded the dependency we had in early childhood? Many men have only to develop a cold in the head for their relationship with their wives to change from dominance to submission, from decisiveness to a childish craving to be looked after; and, as both they and their wives know, this particular change is inimical to the expression of the sexual aspect of their union.

The homosexual male, therefore, cannot make an erotic advance to a woman because he is frightened of her. The most recent research confirms the belief long held by analysts that homosexuality is *faute de mieux*. It is not because men or boys are so overwhelmingly attractive that the homosexual turns to them; but rather because they provide a less dangerous opportunity than do women for the expression of erotic love. As Rado stated, a homosexual adaptation is a result of 'hidden but incapacitating fears of the opposite sex'.

This is, however, not the only aspect. In the chapter on feminine homosexuality we discussed the mechanism of the 'crush'; and we concluded that the irrational attraction which a girl might feel towards an older woman was in part a positive reaching out towards self-discovery and an attempt to find her own femininity. The same is true of homosexual attachments in the male. This positive aspect of homosexuality is seldom emphasized, although its educative value was recognized by the Greeks. We have already stated that in families where the father is indifferent or hostile, the developing boy will neither admire him nor be able to identify with him. In such instances, the boy will often feel a powerful attraction to older men who show an interest in him; for they may be providing him with something which he needs but which has been missing from his home. It is natural enough in any case for the developing boy to have his heroes; they may be older boys at school, masters, or remoter figures like cricketers, astronauts, or television cowboys. Upon such people the boy projects his masculine ideal, his idea of what he himself would like to be; and by identifying himself with these figures, he discovers within himself potentialities of courage, endurance, and whatever other qualities may be considered desirable in the male. Homosexual attachments may often begin with hero-worship; but this is no reason to discourage a growing boy from having his heroes since they play a valuable part in his development and, in the ordinary course of events, he will soon grow out of them.

It is characteristic of this pre-adolescent phase that boys gang up together and shun the company of girls whom they despise as inferior beings. It is a time when affirmation of the male role is being sought; and, just as in primitive societies women are excluded from male initiation rites, so, in our own, there has to be a time when the boy severs his tie with the opposite sex in order to establish himself as male. Women have to be put in their proper place before a man feels strong enough to deal with them; and the exaltation of his own sex combined with the denigration of the opposite sex is part of the process by which a boy emancipates himself from his mother and learns to take his place in the world of men.

The homosexual male has been unable to take this step for the reasons outlined above, and so remains in a condition in which not only are women shunned but in which men remain emotionally important to him. The essential feature of male homosexuality is the persistent adoration of the masculine rather than the feminine. It is the emotional attitude of the boy who looks up to men but cannot feel himself yet to be one of them. People who are unfamiliar with male homosexuality often believe that homosexuals are either posturing, effeminate creatures themselves or else only attracted by men who are obviously of this type. Both assumptions are false. The majority of homosexuals are attracted by men who are particularly rugged, tough, and often exaggeratedly masculine, as can be seen from the photographs of male nudes in those magazines which are supposedly devoted to physical culture, but which are actually designed to exploit the erotic interests of the homosexual. The same exaggerated muscularity can be seen in the figures of the nude male athletes with which Michelangelo decorated the ceiling of the Sistine Chapel. The energy and sense of movement with which these figures are endowed is dependent upon a distortion of male physique. It is a characteristic expression of the homosexual's overvaluation of masculinity, in this instance raised to the level of great art. We worship that which we ourselves do not seem to possess.

Exactly the same tendency is reflected in the homosexual's fascination for the penis. Most youths, whether homosexual or not, show an interest in the comparative size of their own organ, confusing size with functional effectiveness. When heterosexual performance is established, this interest tends to decline. Homosexuals, however, often continue to be obsessed by the penis, and may feel compelled to look at the penises of other men. In some cases the penis acts as a fetish; that is, as a reassuring object, the sight of which provokes or encourages erection. When mutual masturbation has become established, it is natural enough that the penis of another man should become a sexual stimulus for the homosexual: but the compulsion to look at a large penis exists in men who have never put their desires into practice, and is one expression of a more generalized need to search for masculinity which is characteristic of homosexual males. At a primitive level, to be close to someone is to identify oneself with the other person; and the homosexual who searches for a large penis is attempting himself to become the man who possesses this valuable sign of masculine potency. There is evidence to suggest that it is those who are dissatisfied with the size of their penis who are most driven to seek a partner with a large one.

Male homosexuality, therefore, like its female equivalent, can be viewed as a form of emotional immaturity which is dependent upon a failure to become identified with adult membership of one's own sex; and it is characteristic of most homosexuals that they admire masculinity in others, whilst feeling deficient in masculine qualities themselves.

A minority, however, show a preference for men or youths of a softer and more delicate type; pretty boys who conform in appearance, though not necessarily in behaviour, to a feminine stereotype. It seems probable that the homosexual who is attracted by such types of person is really seeking a woman; but, since he fears to make advances to an actual woman for the reasons given above, he chooses a man who most closely approximates to the feminine image. Many homosexuals deny that they have ever experienced any erotic feelings towards women at all; but analytical investigation reveals that some who make such protestations can recall having been aroused sexually in relation to a sister or mother. Manifestly heterosexual dreams are also commonly disclosed by homosexual males, whilst a large proportion have attempted and often achieved heterosexual intercourse at some time during the course of their development.

The belief that a man is necessarily either homosexual or heterosexual in a clear-cut way cannot be substantiated. One quarter of homosexual offences in Great Britain are committed by married men. There are homosexual men whose preferences are so nearly heterosexual that it is easy to imagine that it would require only a modest effort to direct their emotions into the normal channel. Others are frankly bisexual and enjoy sexual relations with both men and women as opportunity offers. Still others prefer a male partner but vicariously enjoy, in phantasy or in reality, the spectacle of the partner having intercourse with a woman, a course which they themselves dare not attempt.

It is often supposed that male homosexuals can be divided into active and passive; the active partner playing the part of the male whilst the passive prefers the feminine role. Such a distinction, however, cannot generally be maintained; for many homosexuals will take either role according to circumstances.

In all homosexual love, there is an element of narcissism. Just as a parent loves his children partly because they spring from himself and resemble himself, so the homosexual loves the person who either is like himself or else seems to be the man he would like to be. One reason why homosexual relationships tend to be unstable is that the couple are so often more competitive with each other than man and wife. The marriages which are most emotionally satisfying and most stable are those in which the male and female roles are clearly demarcated, so that competitive striving is eliminated and each member of the couple can be a complement to the other, rather than a competitor. Few wives enjoy a husband's interference in the kitchen; most husbands prefer to keep their wives out of the office: and there can be little doubt that one of the reasons for the prevalence of divorce is that, since the emancipation and higher education of women, marriage has become a more difficult relationship.

A homosexual couple are less able to define their respective roles satisfactorily than husband and wife. Moreover, since each generally has an inner sense of inferiority as a man, each will be touchier, more liable to take offence and more inclined to be competitive. It is not surprising that male homosexual partnerships are so unstable, and that many homosexual men are incapable of sustaining an emotional relationship with any partner.

This is one of the tragic features of this deviation; for there can be little doubt that much of the homosexual behaviour which causes public concern and against which our laws are directed, springs from simple loneliness. Homosexual behaviour shows a greater tendency than heterosexual behaviour to be compulsive; and those who commit homosexual offences are much more often recidivists than are their heterosexual equivalents. This is so partly because homosexual relationships are seldom fully satisfying. There is always a missing element in homosexual love which causes it to be incomplete. Heterosexual lovers habitually report that the partner with whom they are in love seems to fulfil their lives, to complete them, to make them whole. Homosexual lovers less often repeat such phrases because, inevitably, their love lacks this quality of wholeness. A homosexual man changes partners because he is restlessly on the search for something which he always hopes to find but never quite discovers.

The average man who has a wife to go home to has little idea of the depths of loneliness to which homosexuals can sink, or of the strength of the compulsive urge for sexual contact which drives them. For, in a life which is lonely and frustrating, sex may be the only source of pleasure to which a man can turn and the only certain way of making any emotional contact with another human being. Homosexuals who importune, or who are arrested in public lavatories for making advances to other men may in some instances be self-indulgent lechers. They are far more often unhappy, lonely men driven by a compulsive need to make contact with others which they may deplore but which they cannot wholly control. The self-righteous strictures of judges and magistrates upon such cases reflect a lamentable ignorance of the effects of emotional isolation upon human beings.

Male homosexuality is more of a social problem than lesbianism because it is commoner, because male sexuality is more compulsive, and because in this country the law condemns it. Public opinion is gradually changing towards a more liberal attitude, and it seems probable that sooner or later a government will have the courage to repeal the law which condemns homosexual behaviour between consenting adults. But the homosexual way of life is intrinsically unsatisfying, and we should make every effort to encourage research which will teach us ways of preventing the homosexual pattern from becoming established and of altering it wherever possible.

9 Exhibitionism, Frotteurism, Voyeurism, Buggery

In this chapter, various minor forms of sexual deviation will be discussed which have little in common, save that their practice may bring the person concerned into conflict with the law. Of these deviations, by far the commonest is exhibitionism, or, as the law terms it, indecent exposure. In 1954 2,728 persons were convicted of this offence; and, of the 1,985 sexual offenders studied by the Cambridge Department of Criminal Science, 490 were classified as having committed some form of indecent exposure.

Exhibitionism is the act of exposing the genitals publicly. It is exclusively a male deviation; for, although females may expose the genitals in striptease shows, this is done at the behest of and for the pleasure of others, and is never resorted to by the female as a means of obtaining excitement for herself. Exhibitionism is often, though by no means invariably, a compulsion which recurs again and again in spite of both penalties and treatment. Follow-up studies of those convicted for this offence reveal that, within four years, nineteen per cent have been re-convicted; a rate of re-conviction which is only surpassed by those guilty of homosexual offences against boys.

The majority of those who are prosecuted for indecent exposure are convicted under the Vagrancy Act of 1824 which provides that *every person wilfully, openly, lewdly and obscenely exposing his person with intent to insult any female is a rogue and vagabond*. Although there are other Statutes which do not specify the intent to insult a female, this particular form of words is applicable to the majority of cases of exhibitionism; for, although indecent exposure may take place incidentally as part of a homosexual approach, or simply because of carelessness or a desire to urinate, exhibitionism itself is a heterosexual deviation.

The deviation consists of exposing the penis, usually erect, to passers-by, who may be females of any age, but who, in approximately fifty per cent of cases, are actually under sixteen. This exposure is generally followed by masturbation rather than by any other approach to the females; and it is clear from a consideration of the circumstances and places in which the act occurs that the great majority of men who expose themselves do not intend to make physical contact with the girls and women to whom they display their sexual organs.

The exhibitionist hopes to obtain an emotional reaction from the girls of horror, disgust, or excitement. It is essentially a primitive way of making himself felt as a man. By this crude insistence upon his virility, the exhibitionist hopes to produce a response in a female which will reassure him that, even if he cannot command her love, he may at least be powerful enough to produce some kind of shock in her. As Professor Carstairs said in a recent Reith Lecture, men who expose themselves often claim to be happily married 'but almost invariably they are found to be weak and insecure in their capacity as husbands'. The exhibitionist would rather that he was adversely regarded than not noticed at all; a trait which is familiar in children who, when feeling themselves neglected, often compulsively behave towards adults in a manner so irritating that they invite punishment. The explanation of this behaviour is that even punishment is sometimes preferable to complete indifference; and this is one reason why the exhibitionist, like the neglected child, so commonly fails to respond to legal penalties.

Exhibitionism is, of course, an extremely primitive way of displaying masculinity. Children habitually show an interest in each others' genitals; and it is common in schools and other places for comparisons to be made and measurements taken. The size of the penis is a source of narcissistic satisfaction to most men, and many get pleasure from observing their own genitals in a mirror, and additional pleasure from looking at them when masturbating. The belief that he has large impressive genitals is a sustaining one, especially if a man has no other foundation on which to base his masculine self-esteem: and it is natural for him to think that women will be impressed by them too. However, they seldom are; for women, on the whole, treat the penis as an organ for use rather than for aesthetic admiration, and are seldom as impressed by its magnificence as men would like them to be.

There are, nevertheless, a few women who constantly find that men are exposing themselves to them. These repeated shocks, however, do not have the effect of deterring them from taking solitary walks on heaths and commons where exhibitionists are known to lurk; and the woman who complains that this experience often happens to her may generally be justly accused of seeking it out.

Exhibitionism is so common that all schoolgirls should be told of its occurrence. It is unlikely to disturb girls who are forewarned that it may happen. The only harm that may result is that a child may be frightened by the size of the male organ in the erect state, and may be disturbed by the realization that she was in fact excited by it, and thus keep it as a guilty secret which she feels she must not reveal. But in general, exhibitionism is more of a nuisance than a menace, and should be treated as such.

So much has been made of the fact that exhibitionism tends to be a recidivist offence that it is not generally realized that it is not always a recurrent phenomenon. It is often a regressive substitute; that is, it may be resorted to on only a single occasion, or as a temporary means of satisfaction when other ways of achieving this are denied. Thus, husbands whose wives refuse intercourse during pregnancy, or who have become tired of them, may revert to exhibitionism as a means of relieving tension. It will sometimes be found that this is a repetition of a childhood pattern of behaviour which has been actually used before; but the patient cannot always recall this, and the exhibitionistic urge is one which is so deeply rooted in human nature that it may be assumed to be instinctive rather than learned behaviour.

In this connexion, it is interesting to reflect upon the opportunities for males to exhibit themselves in our civilization in other ways than the primitive manner described above. In earlier periods, male costume frankly drew attention to the genital region, a trend which reached its zenith in the fashion of wearing cod-pieces. These were part of the hose enclosing the penis and testicles which were padded in such a way as to suggest a perpetual erection. But, even when the cod-piece was abandoned, men's breeches tended to be embellished by bows or other devices which might entice the female eye towards the vital area, as can be seen in illustrations of European costume of the fifteenth and sixteenth centuries. In the dress of later periods, the element of erotic display became more generalized or displaced to other regions, but it was not until the end of the eighteenth century that European males ceased to use their costume as a main vehicle for the expression of their exhibitionistic urges. It was probably the trend towards egalitarianism initiated by the French Revolution which resulted in men adopting a more or less uniform style of dress in which opportunity both for display and competition was greatly curtailed. But, especially in recent years, there is still scope for the subtler forms of dandyism; and it is not difficult to detect, in normal males, socially acceptable expressions of that same urge which brings the exhibitionist before a magistrate.

There can be few men who are entirely innocent of any wish to exhibit evidence of their virility. Some men displace their desire for display on to those women who accompany them, requiring them to be elegantly and richly dressed in order to excite the envy of their fellows. Others draw attention to their cars, their bank balances, or their possessions; and, whilst it is true to say that the sexual deviant who exposes himself does so because he is uncertain of his masculinity, it is also certain that most men in higher civilizations require that their masculinity shall not only be felt by themselves but also be displayed to their neighbours, and this is probably as natural to the human male as is the spread of his tail to the peacock.

Exhibitionism is one way of entering upon a sexual exploit which, while involving a member of the opposite sex, does not demand any personal relationship. There are others also. A number of men who find difficulty in making sexual relations of a personal kind engage in the activity known as frotteurism. By this is meant the practice of rubbing the genitals against another person, mostly in a crowd. Such advances, though distasteful to many women, are not always repelled. The focus of interest is usually the buttocks, a part of the feminine body which is apt to be of compulsive, fetishistic interest to many people and which is accessible in crowds in a way in which more intimate portions of female anatomy are not. Frotteurism is seldom a deviation unaccompanied by any other, and is of little importance except in those rare cases where it is strongly compulsive. There can be few men who have not experienced something of the same urge in crowded lifts or other places where they are liable to be pressed up against women. Gratification of this desire, however, renders the person who commits it liable to be convicted of indecent assault upon a female; an offence which may be punished with a sentence of up to two years' imprisonment.

Scoptophilia or voyeurism is another way of obtaining sexual gratification without embarking upon the complexities of a real relationship. The desire to see other people or animals engaging in sexual activity is so widespread that voyeurism cannot possibly be regarded as a sexual deviation unless it has become a main substitute for conventional methods of gratification. In one study, sixty-five per cent of males admitted to having engaged in voyeuristic activity, whilst eighty-three per cent would have liked to do so. Women are less likely to be aroused sexually by visual stimuli; but John Aubrey, the seventeenth-century biographer, records a famous example in his *Brief Lives*. Of Mary Countess of Pembroke, he writes:

She was very salacious, and she had a contrivance that, in the spring of the years, when the stallions were to leap the mares, they were to be brought before such a part of the house, where she had a vidette *to look on them, and please herself with their sport; and then she would act the like sport herself with* her *stallions.*

Striptease shows, and spectacles in which sexual activities are either suggested or actually demonstrated, will always be popular amongst men, whether or not they are leading satisfactory sexual lives; and most men will stop and stare if they have the opportunity of observing a woman undressing. The deliberate seeking out of such opportunities is a substitute sexual activity resorted to by those whose sexual outlets are restricted by circumstance or emotional immaturity. Voyeurs frequently haunt parks in the hope of observing the activities of courting couples, or wander through dark streets at night so that they may peer into lighted bedrooms. Such men provoke complaints from women; but some women invite such attentions by dressing and undressing with needless publicity. Persons indulging in voyeurism are often known as Peeping Toms. In this country, as night walkers or eavesdroppers, they may be bound over by Justices to keep the peace; and in some states of the U.S.A. are liable to imprisonment.

This book has not so far been concerned with the details of physical love-making; for, in the author's opinion, there is no reason to regard any preliminary to coitus as deviant, provided that both lovers enjoy it. It is true that in some cultures mouth-genital contacts have been condemned; but it is mistaken to regard fellatio and cunnilinctus as deviant, since it is rare for either to replace intercourse except amongst homosexuals, and at least sixty per cent of males admit to the practice of one or other activity. In spite of this, in this country, homosexuals who practice fellatio even by mutual consent, are liable to prosecution for gross indecency.

The use of the anal orifice for sexual purposes calls for some comment, however, since the law so ferociously condemns it. *It is felony for a person to commit buggery with another person or with an animal* states the Sexual Offences Act of 1956; and the punishment to which an offender is liable is life imprisonment. The crime consists in inserting the penis into the anal orifice of man or woman; or in having any kind of sexual intercourse with an animal. The former practice is sometimes known as sodomy, the latter as bestiality. In the case of buggery between a man and a woman, each may be equally liable; even when the couple are husband and wife, and each consents to the act. Indeed, according to the letter of the law, any known case of buggery ought to be reported to the police; so that most psychiatrists are breaking the law when they keep silent about the innumerable cases known to them.

That the anal area is erotically sensitive may not be familiar to everyone; but stimulation of the genitals normally causes contraction of the muscles around the anal orifice, and vice versa, and, after orgasm, the anal sphincter can be seen to open and close convulsively. Both men and women may be capable of reaching orgasm as a result of anal stimulation; and there is no doubt that some people enjoy being penetrated by this route.

Anal intercourse is most commonly practised between homosexual males since, for them, the choice of bodily orifice is more restricted than for heterosexuals. It used to be thought that homosexual males could be divided into active and passive on the basis of which role they preferred in anal intercourse; but many in fact play either part as the occasion demands. The practice of sodomy is not confined to homosexuals. There are a number of men who prefer anal intercourse in heterosexual relations. The unsophisticated use this kind of intercourse as a method of birth control which saves both expense and preparation, but in other cases the reasons are more complicated. In an earlier chapter, we discussed the so-called castration complex, and the fear which many men have of penetrating the vagina, which they regard as dangerous. To some of these men, the anal orifice is less alarming, and this is one reason for its use. In one case known to the author of a man who wished, but who did not dare, to have anal intercourse, the castration complex was particularly evident, since he had a generalized apprehension of being engulfed, and could not even put his finger into a sea anemone without alarm.

To other men, the anal orifice is attractive because they childishly associate sex with excretion, and become erotically aroused at the idea of experiencing a pleasure which is associated with a forbidden area. There is some dispute amongst analysts as to whether Freud's description of the anal stage of development is accurate; but there is no doubt that there are many people for

whom excretion and the organs connected with it have a deep
emotional significance. The Marquis de Sade, whose multiple
perversions would have lost much of their charm for him if he
had not been a moralist, preferred sodomy, because its practice
seemed closer than vaginal intercourse to the 'wickedness' upon
which his heart was set.

English law, in prescribing so severe a penalty for an act
which, although aesthetically unattractive, seems between consenting adults to be harmless, is reflecting a prejudice which is
both ecclesiastical and medieval; for, throughout the middle ages,
sodomy and heresy were closely linked. Even today, however,
certain persons seem to regard anal intercourse with a kind of
fascinated horror; and, in February 1962, the Warden of All
Souls wrote a long article in *Encounter* in which he endeavoured
to demonstrate that certain passages in *Lady Chatterley's Lover*
described the act. The Warden believed that, if the jury had
realized this, they would not have permitted the publication of
D. H. Lawrence's novel; but it is also reasonable to suppose
that not everyone finds the practice of sodomy either as shocking
or worth as much detailed attention as the Warden gives to it.

Bestiality, the other form of buggery which is forbidden by
English law, consists in the use of animals as sexual objects. Most
cases occur in rural districts, where farm labourers have been
known to have intercourse with a wide variety of domestic
animals. Cases have also been recorded of women having sexual
relations with dogs and with other animals; but this is rare
except in the case of exhibitions put on by prostitutes to entertain
their clients. Bestiality is a sexual deviation which seldom comes
under the direct scrutiny of the psychiatrist as an actual practice.
Phantasies in which women are seduced by animals are, however,
familiar to everyone; for who has not seen a picture of Leda and
the Swan, or, at least, a cinema poster of some fearsome ape
bearing away a woman in his arms? To the imagination, the
animal represents sexuality freed from the restrictions imposed by
civilization and humanity; and both men and women envy the
abandon with which an animal may be supposed to satisfy its
erotic needs. The chief interest which attaches to both sodomy

and bestiality is not the practice of these acts but the savage penalties which the law attaches to them. Man's cruelty to man is surely more remarkable and shocking a phenomenon than his various forms of sexual activity.

Paedophilia

The seduction of female children by adults is generally regarded with a horror which precludes rational discussion; and when there is a report in the press of the rape of a little girl, many people who are generally of a kindly disposition demand flogging, execution, or at least life imprisonment for the offender. Fortunately, cases of rape or of actual bodily harm to children as a result of a sexual advance are extremely rare, and the attention which such cases attract is out of all proportion to their frequency. It is presumably because of the high value which society attaches to female virginity that it is assaults upon girls which most shock the public. The seduction of boys, although deplored, and although often thoroughly reported in the Sunday newspapers, does not usually arouse such violent emotion. If it did so, the waiting lists for entry to our public schools would hardly be so long as they now are.

The sexual advances which are made to children usually take the form of verbal approaches or genital exhibition, or may consist of fondling the child without any specifically genital contact. In a small proportion there is caressing of the child's genital organs or an attempt to persuade the child to manipulate the genitals of the adult. Actual sexual intercourse is now extremely rare: although, in the past, the procuring of children was not uncommon, and, as recently as 1885, the journalist W. T. Stead was able to buy a girl of thirteen for £10 and keep her in a brothel. We owe it to his articles describing this that procuring girls for prostitution became an indictable offence in this country.

There is no doubt that some libertines, who have tasted and perhaps tired of every other sexual pleasure, will turn to children in the hope of restoring a flagging sexual appetite, and child prostitution is still common in the East, as it was in this country a century ago.

But some apparently normal men, under stress of sexual deprivation, or when judgement and self-control have been impaired by brain damage or by alcohol, are capable of making sexual advances to children. Guy de Maupassant's story *The Roque Child* is an entirely convincing, imaginative reconstruction of how this could happen to a man who is normally upright and controlled. In the story the Mayor of a village who has been recently widowed is tormented by unfulfilled desire. When he accidentally comes across a pubescent girl of twelve bathing naked in the woods, his emotions overcome his scruples and he assaults her. She weeps and screams; and to stop her cries he puts his hands around her throat, killing her unintentionally. The story ends with the Mayor's suicide from remorse; and it is a tribute to Maupassant's skill and imaginative sympathy that we are able to feel compassion for the man who could perform an act which in itself is dreadful, but which might be committed by many of us if the provocation was sufficient.

As distinct from such behaviour in more or less normal people, a sexual deviation in which a man or a woman is exclusively attracted to children is fortunately uncommon. Nevertheless, there is always a small number of people who do feel a compulsive attraction of this kind; and although by far the majority of these people never attempt to satisfy their desires except in phantasy, a few are unable entirely to control a tendency in themselves of which they are usually bitterly ashamed. Paedophilia, as the sexual love of children is sometimes called, is a deviation which occurs in both heterosexual and homosexual men. There are some women who also prefer their lovers to be much younger than themselves, but it is uncommon for a woman to be accused of interfering sexually with children of either sex. In a recent case, however, a twenty-year-old wife was accused, though acquitted, of a sexual association with an eleven-year-old schoolboy; and, in law, a woman can be guilty of indecent assault on either male or female. However, the desire for children as a truly compulsive, deviant urge seems, like the majority of sexual deviations, to be a male prerogative.

The man who suffers from paedophilia as a true deviation does not do so from excess of sensuality, but rather because he has been unable to find sexual satisfaction in an adult relationship. It is not from a superfluity of lust, but rather because of a timid inability to make contact with contemporaries that a man generally finds that children form the focus of his sexual interest.

In the chapter on sado-masochism, we discussed how it was that a man who was uncertain of himself as a man could become reassured and therefore potent if he created a situation in which he dominated his partner. Faced with another adult, he might feel that it was only when she had submitted to being beaten or in some way humiliated, that he could fulfil the masculine role. Confronted with a child, however, he would hardly need such devices to ensure his dominance; for a child, being smaller and weaker, would be more likely to yield to him and would be also less of a threat to his superiority. In the chapter on fetishism, some of the fears which men have of women were discussed, and it was pointed out that a man who had not freed himself from the maternal tie tended to regard women as dangerous and potentially 'castrating'. One way of circumventing such fears is to substitute a child for an adult woman.

Moreover, the child is more easily impressed; and the man who believes that no woman would ever admire him may hope that children will accord him the esteem which he has failed to win from those of his own age. There are actually many adults who only feel at ease with children, whether or not they have any sexual interest in them: and most people will number among their acquaintances someone who is brusque and difficult in ordinary social relations, but who can be relaxed and playful with small children in a way which seems entirely alien to his usual prickly exterior. Lewis Carroll, who incidentally had a penchant for photographing little girls in the nude, was clearly a person who was much more himself with children than with people of his own age and status.

Since the seduction of children is looked upon with disgust by the majority of adults reared in the West, it is a crime which has a special appeal for those who have a compulsion to act upon the very worst impulses which they can discover within themselves. Such masochistic individuals feel compelled to commit crimes in order to obtain first punishment and then forgiveness. Dostoievsky seems to have belonged to this group; and is said to have confessed to Turgenev that he once violated a little girl who was brought to him in a bath-house. Unfortunately this revelation produced neither the horror nor the sympathy which Dostoievsky looked for, since Turgenev retained the impassive exterior which befits a gentleman or, nowadays, an analyst; and Dostoievsky rushed out of the room in a temper. Whether or not his confession was true, it seems certain that he was preoccupied with paedophilia; for Svidrigaylov in *Crime and Punishment* is guilty of it; and in a chapter of *The Possessed* which the publisher refused to print, Stavrogin confesses to the same offence. The compulsion to act out one's most deplorable impulses is not, however, a common reason for the seduction of children.

Children are both less demanding and more ready to give affection than adults, so that the man who believes that he will be inadequate to a woman's demands upon him, or who cannot believe that he can inspire a woman's love, is more likely to turn towards children. Children are easily pleased with small gifts of sweets or money, and more often show affection towards the donor in instances where an adult might be suspicious.

When sexual impulses are denied their normal fulfilment in an adult love relationship they continue to seek expression in ways which are generally abandoned by those who have been able to reach a more mature stage of development. Very many people have been paedophilics in one sense; for very many people have had sexual contacts with children when they themselves were children. When adult sexual expression has never been attained, the desire for sexual contact with children may persist. When an adult relation has had to be abandoned, because of death, absence, or illness of a partner, the desire for sexual contact with children may re-assert itself.

Often, the period when the physical maturation of adolescence is just beginning seems to have a special fascination. The desire for a pubescent girl may be simply the desire for a virgin; and virginity appeals to men because it reassures them by demonstrating that there have been no prior competitors. But the spectacle of emergent youth also recalls to many people that exciting period of their lives when their own vague yearnings became crystallized into a genital orgasm. Partly through a vicarious identification with the adolescent, they hope to recall the rapture of such pristine experience; and thus find excitement in talking to adolescents about their sexual experiences, in giving them information about sex, and in introducing or suggesting various sexual practices. The man who is always on the school bus and who leads the friendly conversation around from biology lessons to 'crushes', to kisses in the dark, and then to masturbation, must be familiar to many schoolgirls. Such men have much in common with exhibitionists, since part of the excitement which they are seeking is derived from the hope that they may have the power to shock or horrify.

The desire to recapture some experience of the past is especially characteristic of the homosexual seduction of boys. In the chapter on male homosexuality, it was postulated that the pretty boy might be the nearest approach to a woman which the homosexual could desire without anxiety. In many instances, however, the boy is attractive because he represents some aspect of the man's own youthful past. As we have already said, homosexual love contains a strong element of narcissism. That is, in loving another man, the homosexual is admiring himself or what he would like to be himself. Similarly, in loving a boy, a man may be admiring the boy he would like to have been or actually was. Homosexual schoolmasters often have an especially tender feeling for tough, adventurous boys: and a similar emotion can be detected in many youth leaders, prison visitors, and welfare workers who evince a particular interest in delinquent youths. Such boys are fascinating to those who themselves possess an unruly, rebellious streak which they have never dared to admit or act upon.

Another aspect of the seduction of youth is the wish to give the boy or girl affection which the man himself would like to have had in childhood. The desire to make up for what was missing from their own youth is characteristic of many parents, who are often unwisely lavish in giving their children what they themselves felt that they lacked. In seeking to play the role of a generous parent towards a child for whom he may entertain a sincere regard, the lonely adult may easily find himself proceeding from an affectionate embrace to a more intimately sensual caress.

It is so far taken for granted that the seduction of children by adults is undesirable that it may seem otiose to discuss its actual effects. Most people assume that it is necessarily harmful; but various authorities who have examined children who have been seduced have concluded that the emotional as opposed to the physical damage which is done to children is more the result of adult horror than of anything intrinsically dreadful in the sexual contact itself. As Kinsey says;

When children are constantly warned by parents and teachers against contacts with adults, and when they receive no explanation of the exact nature of the forbidden contact, they are ready to become hysterical as soon as any older person approaches them or stops and speaks to them in the street, or fondles them, or proposes to do anything for them, even though the adult may have had no sexual objective in mind. Some of the more experienced students of juvenile problems have come to believe that the emotional reactions of the parents, police officers, and other adults who discover that a child has had such a contact, may disturb the child more seriously than the sexual contacts themselves.

The distaste which most people feel for the seduction of children is based on the supposition that the situation is bound to be one in which love is reduced to lust and in which the adult seeks satisfaction at the expense of the child without regard to the latter's feelings. This is not invariably the case; and in some instances in which there has been repeated sexual contact between the child and the adult the child has been eager to continue the association and has showed no signs of disturbance until discovered and reprimanded. Such children are reported to possess unusually charming personalities and to be able to make particularly easy personal contacts.

There is no doubt that, in the past, far too much emphasis has been placed upon childhood seduction as a cause of subsequent neurosis; and parents may be reassured to know that many children survive such incidents without showing evidence of emotional disturbance in later life. Nevertheless, sexual contacts between adults and children are certainly much more likely to upset the child than are similar activities with its contemporaries; and society is right to abhor and to forbid such contacts. In Chapter 1 it was suggested that, ideally, sexual relations should be an exchange between partners who felt themselves to be on equal terms; and it has been affirmed in other chapters that many adults' sexual difficulties are best explained in terms of the persistence of childhood fears that the partner is more powerful and therefore frightening.

When one partner is in reality both larger and more dominant there is a strong risk that any erotic advance which he makes may seem to the child to be an assault rather than an expression of affection; and, even if the adult does not actively use force, the child may become frightened that he will do so. To small children, adults who are in any way uncontrolled are likely to be frightening, whether they are angry, drunk, or sexually excited. There is, therefore, a danger that, as a result of sexual contacts with adults, sex will become unnecessarily frightening to the child and may interfere with its capacity to enjoy love-making in later life. This is particularly likely to happen if the adult who makes the overture is the child's parent, and most psychiatrists will have seen cases of frigidity in women which resulted from an incestuous advance on the part of the father. It is not difficult to produce a condition in a girl in which any subsequent advance from a male is repudiated because it is regarded as an attack rather than an invitation to pleasure.

If the seduction of a child does not result in the implantation of a fear of sexuality, it may cause the premature arousal of desire which the child then finds it hard to fulfil. Some children, especially after a long-continued sexual association with an adult, become deprived and emotionally disturbed when such an association ends: and, when they grow up, may be led to repeat the pattern by themselves seducing another child. This was so in the case of a young man who once consulted the author on account of a sexual interest in boys of which he felt much ashamed. He had himself been seduced by a male friend of the family in pre-adolescence, and had continued this association for several years, partly out of a genuine affection for the man, who in some degree compensated for the deficiencies of his own father. When he himself grew up, he found that he was assailed by the desire to do to another boy what had been done to him.

Although the fears which parents feel for their children are often exaggerated, and the harm which is done to a child by an adult's sexual advance is seldom severe, the risk of emotional damage is always present, and the need which society feels to protect children from such advances is therefore justified. But we are still a long way from the ideal method of dealing with either the child victim or the adult perpetrator of such an assault. For the child needs protection, not only from the person who has assaulted it, but from the emotional disturbances of the surrounding adults, and from the distressing experience of having to give evidence in a public court if a charge is brought. Parents sometimes fail to report instances in which a child has been interfered with sexually since they realize that the police procedure of obtaining a statement, however gently undertaken, and the subsequent ordeal of having to give evidence on intimate matters in court may be more disturbing to the child than the original incident. In Israel special measures have been taken in order to keep children under the age of fourteen out of court. Youth Examiners have been appointed whose task it is to interview children who are alleged to have been the victims of sexual offences, and also to investigate the home background of the child and interview the parents. Most of these Examiners are women who are trained in psychiatric social work or allied specialities and their report is admissible as evidence in court. This procedure is not only a protection to the child, but may also be fairer to the accused person. For it is well known that children, especially small children, are poor witnesses, who often fail to distinguish fact from phantasy, and who are very liable to say what they think is required from them rather than to give an account of what actually occurred. Moreover, certain adolescent or pre-adolescent girls have been known to make wholly false accusations that men made sexual approaches to them, based on nothing more than their own sexual phantasies and a desire to make themselves conspicuous. Such false accusations may not stand up to cross-examination in court; but it is often difficult for a jury to believe that an attractive, innocent-looking thirteen-year-old girl is capable of such deceit. There are objections to the admissibility of using hearsay evidence; and it may also be considered unfair not to give an accused person the chance of cross-examining his accuser. The whole question of sexual assaults upon children needs re-examination in the light of modern knowledge both from the point of view of the child and also of his assailant. The adult who makes a sexual assault upon a child requires medical and psychiatric investigation rather than punishment. The older man who commits such an offence for the first time is very often suffering from cerebral arteriosclerosis or some other organic affliction which has damaged his brain and impaired his control. The younger person who feels a compulsive attraction towards children does so as a result of a disorder of his emotional development which may be treatable by psychotherapy, but which in any case is most unlikely to be influenced by punishment. Sexually deviant people are already burdened with an excessive load of guilt and inferiority, and to punish them by imprisonment without treatment is likely to increase, rather than to diminish the chance of their offence being repeated.

11   Methods of Treatment

Of all psychiatric conditions, the sexual deviations are most obviously to be attributed to nurture rather than to nature. Whilst it is possible to argue, as many do, that homosexuality is an inborn rather than an acquired condition, it is hard to maintain the same of fetishism, of transvestism, or of other deviations which are clearly connected with the early experiences and influences of childhood. One can postulate that sexually deviant people may possess some genetic defect of a general kind which interferes with their capacity to reach emotional maturity; for the various forms of deviation undoubtedly demonstrate a partial failure of the individual to achieve a fully adult sexual status. But, to date, there is little convincing evidence to support the hypothesis of any inborn inferiority, and no reason to suppose that, in any other respect, sexually deviant persons are less intelligent or less admirable than their more orthodox neighbours. Nor, as has repeatedly been pointed out, can any hard and fast line be drawn between the deviant and the normal; for in everybody embryonic forms of several deviations can be detected.

It is hard to believe, therefore, that any form of sexual deviation is likely to be eliminated by eugenic measures: but it is certainly probable that, if the wisdom and tolerance of parents increases, children are less likely to experience the extremes of sexual guilt and inferiority which are the usual prerequisites for the development of these disorders. It is not unreasonable to hope that the children of today may be less tormented by, and therefore more able to accept, their sexual impulses than were their grandfathers;

and thus less liable to the distortions of emotional development which result in sexual deviation.

Since sexual deviations appear to be the result chiefly of psychological stress and the emotional conditioning of childhood, it is reasonable to suppose that any treatment of the adults who suffer from these disorders which is attempted, should be based on an endeavour to reverse or at least undo these harmful influences. Not much result can be expected from the use of tranquillizers, of electro-convulsive therapy, of insulin coma, or of whatever transient fad of physical therapy may be occupying the attention of enthusiasts in this field; for, although such methods may have their place in calming anxiety or inducing changes of mood, they cannot be expected to relieve long-standing feelings of guilt and inferiority, or permanently to improve the sufferer's relationship with his fellow men. These latter aims can often be attained by analytical psychotherapy of a kind which enables the patient to attain a new and better attitude to himself and his problems by means of the relationship which he achieves with the therapist. But, before proceeding to describe the psychotherapy of sexual deviations, we must discuss those instances in which long-term psychotherapy is either inappropriate or unnecessary, and also some of the other methods of treatment which have been attempted.

First come the cases in which the deviation is expressed or acted upon only because the patient's normal degree of self-control is impaired, either temporarily or permanently. Everyone is familiar with the fact that, under the influence of alcohol, a man may perform actions which he would not carry out if sober. When his brain is poisoned or damaged, a man cannot fully control his behaviour, and is more likely to act upon impulses which are usually suppressed or which may be so deeply buried that the man himself is scarcely aware of their existence. Thus, a middle-aged homosexual had twice, during the course of an otherwise blameless life, been in trouble with the police for soliciting. Many years separated the two offences, each of which was committed under the influence of alcohol. In such a case, treatment should be primarily directed towards stopping the man drinking, and only secondarily towards the sexual deviation, for which he was in any case not seeking help.

Analytical psychotherapy is also inappropriate in those rather common cases in which an elderly man for the first time commits a sexual offence, such as exposing himself or an assault upon a child. The middle-aged and elderly are increasingly likely to suffer from various chronic diseases which damage the brain and which impair self-control permanently, in the same way as does alcohol temporarily; and alcohol itself may result in permanent harm if taken in sufficient quantities for long enough. Arteriosclerosis, the various forms of senile and pre-senile dementia, and general paralysis of the insane, are examples of diseases which cause an actual loss of brain substance or an interference with the nutrition of the brain cells such that conscious control is lessened and the emergence of underlying emotional tendencies facilitated. There is not a single one of us who can be sure that, in his latter years, he will not become the subject of a paragraph in the *News of the World*. For all of us harbour within us deviant sexual impulses, and all of us are subject to those processes of disease and decay which may release such tendencies. It is clear that the treatment of a man of sixty-five who commits a sexual offence as a result of cerebral arteriosclerosis must be very different to that which we would hope to give a young man in trouble on the same account.

Sexually deviant behaviour can, therefore, result from brain disease or brain damage, and it is important to ascertain whether such conditions are present, especially in cases where an offence has been committed, since a man cannot be held responsible for behaviour which he is unable to control because of physical disease. It will generally be found in such cases that there is other evidence of brain disease besides the sexually deviant behaviour – loss of memory for recent events, episodes of confusion and disorientation, some degree of speech disorder, or electroencephalographic changes – and although damaged brain cells cannot be replaced, it is possible to help a number of these unfortunate people with medical and social measures, designed to protect both themselves and society from further transgressions against the social code.

It is also important to distinguish those cases in which sexually deviant behaviour or impulse is a temporary result of an unusual situation. We have already stated that, when a person's normal sexual outlet is blocked, his sexual impulse will tend to regress; that is, to seek expression in ways which he had abandoned, perhaps many years previously. A happily married man may, during his wife's pregnancy, make advances to a child; another, on losing his wife, may expose himself for the first time. In these cases, there may certainly be some degree of failure in sexual maturation, since the average man does not necessarily turn to a childish sexual practice directly he is deprived of his normal outlet. Yet, the important feature of such cases is not the deviation but the deprivation which led to the deviation being expressed; and, if the latter can be remedied, the deviant behaviour will tend to disappear.

Occasionally, too, people who are subject to severe attacks of depression complain that, during the period when they are depressed, they become the prey of deviant sexual impulses which do not ordinarily trouble them. Anyone who is severely depressed tends to regress emotionally, to become more dependent and less able to make a normal relationship with other people. Thus, in depression, the stage is set for the resuscitation of childish sexual phantasies and practices and, in such instances, the important thing is to treat the person's depression first, rather than the sexual deviation which may well disappear when the depression lifts.

Obviously, too, there exist cases where it is more important to alter the person's environment than to try and alter the person. Homosexual behaviour is more prevalent in circumstances where the opposite sex is not available, or in situations where there is a long-standing tradition of homosexuality, as there is in certain colleges. A boy of nineteen or twenty who has had an active homosexual career at school and who is worried that he may remain homosexual rather than progress to involvement with girls, will be well advised not to enter the Navy, or if he is attracted by boys, to take up schoolmastering. Similarly, it will be found that many mental defectives will respond better to rather authoritarian forms of treatment and to control of the environment rather than to analytical psychotherapy, for they cannot be expected fully to take responsibility for their own impulses.

The treatment of juveniles who show deviant sexual behaviour, or who commit sexual offences need seldom be prolonged; for the majority respond well to guidance, explanation, and the kind of emotional support which can be given in relatively few interviews. A recent study of twenty-nine boys who had committed sexual misdemeanours showed that the subsequent development of twenty-one was satisfactory. The serious view which parents and other authorities so often take of these cases is seldom justified.

The persistent sexual offender presents a special, though relatively minor, problem to which, at present, there is no satisfactory solution. The report of the Cambridge Department of Criminal Science on Sexual Offences, to which reference has already been made, disclosed that persistent sexual offenders are rare. Only three per cent of all those who had been convicted on sexual charges had three or more previous convictions for sexual offences. The commonest sexual offence to be persistently repeated is the trivial one of indecent exposure; but there also exist a few individuals who are repeatedly convicted for offences against children. Such persons are sometimes mentally defective; but even those who are of high intelligence may be so compulsively driven by their impulses that they do not respond well to psychotherapy or to any other form of treatment. Various attempts have therefore been made to treat such men by actually reducing the strength of their sexual drive rather than by attempting to help them to control it or to alter its direction. The methods employed to do this have been the administration of hormones, and the operation of castration. The administration of female sex hormones (oestrogens) to males has the effect of suppressing the activity of the testicular glands, and thus diminishing both the production of spermatozoa, and also the strength of the sexual drive. However, this type of 'medical castration' is difficult to apply, since it depends upon the subject's perseverence in taking tablets. Most of the cases in which this treatment is considered are of men who show less than normal foresight and control, and who cannot necessarily be expected to cooperate in a treatment which they may in any case resent. There are also most serious disadvantages. Oestrogens affect not only the testes; they may also cause nausea, obesity, and an embarrassing enlargement of the breasts. Kinsey goes so far as to say:

Since an excessive supply of estrogens may affect many functions besides sexual behaviour, and since an excessive supply may do irreparable damage to other glandular structures, several research endocrinologists assert that they consider the use of estrogens to lower the sexual responsiveness of a male nothing less than medical malpractice.

The surgical operation of castration has been fairly extensively carried out on sexual recidivists, especially in Scandinavia. However, adult males who have been castrated may still remain capable of erection and orgasm; and the operation does not always prevent the repetition of the offence and the reconviction of the offender. In most countries where the operation has been performed it has been carried out only with the consent of the subject; although such consent may not be as 'voluntary' as it appears, since earlier release from gaol or hospital may be promised to those who agree to it. Even when their consent has been obtained, a proportion of the castrated become and remain embittered and resentful. In Germany, where the operation was made legally compulsory, the results appear to have been worse than those achieved in Scandinavia; a fact which indicates that the results of castration cannot be assessed in terms of its physical effect alone, and that the willingness of the offender to cooperate is an essential factor in even surgical attempts to modify his behaviour.

It is hardly to be expected that the reduction of an individual's sexual drive would necessarily result in the disappearance of certain compulsive forms of deviant behaviour. For, as has been pointed out throughout this book, homosexuality, paedophilia, and other forms of sexual deviation are not merely ways of obtaining physical gratification, but also subserve the deviant individual's need for companionship, for admiration, or even for the restoration of self-esteem by inviting punishment. These emotional needs, which are rather indirectly connected with the strength of the sexual drive itself, are not likely to be profoundly altered by the latter's diminution.

As a Lord Chief Justice pointed out in a recent case, the basic fact is that the results of surgical castration are unpredictable. It therefore seems very doubtful whether this drastic operation is ever justified. The psychological result is often to impair the self-esteem of the subject still further, and to make it still more difficult for him to achieve normal relations with others: his compulsive sexual behaviour is not necessarily prevented; and the mutilation inflicted upon him is irrevocable. Although favourable results have been reported, especially from Denmark, there is a great deal to be said against making castration into a legally recognized method of treatment in this country. As one writer has put it; 'In this country research and not legislation is needed for sex crimes.'

Recidivist offenders form a very small proportion of the cases of sexual deviation which come to the notice of psychiatrists, and there is no need to consider their treatment further here except to reiterate the futility of giving repeated short prison sentences to such people. Society must be protected; but the ordinary prison is not the place in which to confine homosexuals, or indeed any other sexual deviant, for they merely become confirmed in their deviation. It is to be hoped that the opening of the new institution for mentally abnormal criminals will prompt research into ways of helping those few sexual deviants who repeatedly break the law.

The majority of persons suffering from sexual deviation who consult a psychiatrist do not fall into the categories which we have so far considered in this chapter. Most will require some form of psychotherapy, and this, ideally, should be of the analytical variety which will be discussed in the next chapter. Hypnosis and other methods of psychotherapy based on suggestion have only a limited place in the treatment of sexual deviation, although a few highly suggestible patients may respond to some extent. A boy on the point of abandoning homosexuality for the pursuit of girls can be encouraged in this course by suggestion, which in any case is bound to enter into any form of psychotherapy. But compulsive obsessional symptoms, of which most deviant phantasies and practices are examples, seldom respond to hypnosis. This is partly because such symptoms are not superficial excrescences, but are deeply rooted in the person's character structure; and partly because people who suffer from such symptoms generally belong to the kind of introverted, obsessional type who responds poorly to hypnosis and direct suggestion.

Recently, psychologists who are dissatisfied with the unproven and complex hypotheses of psychoanalysis, have attempted to substitute for it a type of treatment which is called behaviour therapy. This treatment is based on the theory of conditioned reflexes springing from the work of Pavlov, and upon research into the processes of learning. In the chapter on fetishism, we postulated that one factor in the development of this disorder was a tendency to be easily conditioned by sexual stimuli. Behaviour therapy aims a direct attack upon the conditioned response, and has been applied to the treatment of various forms of sexual deviation. The principle of the treatment is to induce a distaste for the object which has become sexually exciting, whether it be a fetish or a person of inappropriate age or sex; and this is done by associating the object with an unpleasant experience, such as vomiting. This form of behaviour therapy, known as aversion therapy, was originally used in the treatment of alcoholism. The patient was given alcohol and, at the same time, injections of apomorphine to induce vomiting. After several repetitions, the mere idea of taking alcohol may cause the patient to feel sick, and may therefore help him to avoid alcohol.

Aversion therapy has been used with some success in cases of homosexuality, of transvestism, and of fetishism; but it is too early yet to say whether it is a permanently effective treatment, or what disadvantages may accompany it. It is probably best to regard it as an adjunct to, rather than a replacement for, psychotherapy. Since it aims only to cure the particular symptom without reference to the patient's personality as a whole, it cannot be a treatment which will replace psychotherapy. For although the first aim of patients who seek psychotherapy may be to find relief from their symptoms, they are also seeking understanding, compassion, and the possibility of improving their human relationships in general; and no treatment which leaves these intangibles out of account is likely to meet their need.

When considering any form of treatment for a sexual deviation, it is essential to consider both the person as a whole and also the circumstances in which he finds himself. There is no specific in the sense in which one might prescribe insulin in the case of diabetes. Of course, many, perhaps most, sexually deviant people do not seek treatment. Some do not realize that there is any treatment available; others do not believe that such treatment could ever be effective; whilst many are too ashamed of their condition to reveal it to any other person unless circumstances compel them to do so.

Some patients come to a psychiatrist because their desires have brought them into conflict with the law or are sent by magistrates, probation officers, or other officials: but many voluntarily and spontaneously seek treatment because they feel themselves to be the prey of phantasies and impulses which they fear and shun, but of which they cannot rid themselves. Some people find it hard to understand that one can harbour thoughts and feelings within oneself which are distasteful but which one cannot banish. They cling to the illusion that everything mental is under their voluntary control. But nearly everyone has at times had a tune running in their head which will not depart, or an unpleasant thought or picture which cannot be brought under conscious control. Many, especially in childhood, have felt compelled to walk in the squares on the pavement, to count steps, to touch wood, or to carry out some other ritual act which is known to be unreasonable. Others are frightened of saying the wrong thing on social occasions, since they discover to their chagrin that it is just when it would be most inappropriate that the wrong thing always seems on the tip of their tongue. The phenomenon of finding oneself surprised or shocked by the contents of one's own mind, even when fully conscious, is a familiar one; and even those who cannot recall this waking experience are likely to remember dreams of sensuality or violence which they would hesitate to accept as reflecting their own inner nature.

It cannot be too often reiterated that sexually deviant persons do not consciously choose to be so. The impulses and phantasies which beset them are not the result of deliberation or voluntary choice, but are as much outside the realm of conscious control as is a dream. This is not to say that a man has no choice as to whether or not he acts upon his impulses. The man who is transvestite or homosexual cannot help feeling as he does; but whether he actually dresses up or makes advances to young men is under his control to some extent, as is the normal sexual impulse in the average person. The degree to which normal sexual impulses are controllable is, however, generally over-estimated; especially by self-righteous and elderly persons in positions of authority. It is difficult to say whether or not deviant sexual impulses are more importunately compulsive than the hetero-sexual drive of the ordinary male. It is quite possible that they are; since, for the reasons already discussed, deviant sexual practices seldom bring full sexual satisfaction, and the sufferer is therefore in a more permanent state of erotic tension than those who are more able to satisfy themselves. At any rate, there is no reason to believe that deviant sexuality is any less compulsive than the normal variety; and those who condemn sexual deviants for lack of self-control should try to recall their own adolescent history. Sexuality is an impersonal and extremely powerful instinctive drive which seeks expression irrespective of the conscious will of the individual. It is safe to assume that those men who claim to be able entirely to control or suppress the expression of sex, at any rate while they are still in the first half of life, are actually undersexed. Reformed rakes do exist; but it is not until age has somewhat diminished their sexual capacities that the reform is generally accomplished.

When a pattern of sexual outlet has been established in

adolescence, it will usually be continued for many years, even though the circumstances of the individual may radically alter. A man who is used to experiencing orgasm two or three times a week is likely to go on doing so, although the ways in which his sexuality finds expression may vary. As Kinsey has shown, the average man who has lost a wife through death or divorce continues to lead almost as active a sexual life as when he was married. In men, though not in most women, the need for a sexual outlet is so imperious that, like the need for food, it cannot be regarded as being wholly within the power of the individual to control.

Sexually deviant people who seek psychiatric treatment, and who are judged to be suitable cases for psychotherapy of some kind, present problems which in some aspects differ from those displayed in other psychiatric cases. A person suffering from depression or claustrophobia may be assumed to wish whole-heartedly to rid himself of his symptoms. The position of the sexual deviant is more equivocal. For, although he may genuinely deplore his sadism or his homosexuality, his deviation does bring him some instinctual release, and therefore gives pleasure as well as pain. Claustrophobia is seldom anything but a disadvantage; but a masturbatory phantasy of beating adolescent girls is exciting and partially satisfying, however much the man who suffers from such phantasies may wish that he did not. It is generally agreed, therefore, that the psychotherapy of a sexual deviation is apt to be a more complicated and difficult undertaking than that of a condition in which the symptoms give no pleasure; for the patient is bound to be somewhat ambivalent towards getting rid of it. In the psychotherapy of anxiety states, the therapist is generally dealing with a person whose instinctual impulses are inadequately expressed. As Fenichel puts it, 'Neurotics are persons whose real actions are blocked.' In the sexual deviations, a person's real actions are also blocked, but the deviation represents an action which is a partial substitute for the real thing. For example, the homosexual who makes advances to small boys is using them as a substitute for women; and the exhibitionist is substituting the exposure of the genitals for intercourse. Sexually deviant people suffer from the damming back of the stream of their libido, just as do anxiety neurotics; but their deviation is a tortuous and indirect channel for part of the stream which has circumvented the dam.

It must be frankly acknowledged that, at present, psychotherapy which is sufficiently skilled and sufficiently prolonged to be of substantial benefit is not available to the majority of people who suffer from either sexual deviations or other forms of psychological disturbance. As a psychiatrist wrote recently in *The Twentieth Century*:

The facilities available under the National Health Service for the treatment of neurosis are inadequate and unsatisfactory at all levels. . . . The management of neurosis must be the only branch of medicine where there is about the same amount of treatment carried out privately as under the N.H.S.; there can be little doubt, too, that the quality of private care is better than that of N.H.S. care. This is not because privately practising psychiatrists are better, but because they can devote more time to individual patients.

To pay for private treatment is far beyond the means of most people, since a year's analytical treatment may cost between six and seven hundred pounds. Moreover, there are not nearly enough psychiatrists available to meet the needs of the population. It is possible to argue that the demand for psychotherapy expands *pari passu* with the provision of psychiatrists to meet it; and no one wants to see a society in this country in which people habitually turn to psychiatrists when suffering from the minor emotional disturbances which afflict us all, or when making any decision about their lives. The fact remains, however, that we are hardly beginning to provide adequate care for neurotic disorders, and that the supply of psychotherapy falls woefully short of the demand.

12 Treatment by Analytical Psychotherapy

This chapter describes the principles upon which, in the author's view, the analytical psychotherapy of the sexual deviations should be based. The fact that such treatment is not easily available because of the time and money involved, and because of the shortage of trained psychotherapists, has already been deplored. In what follows it is assumed that the patient is sincerely seeking help for himself and that the psychotherapist is able to give him sufficient time to deal effectively with his condition.

The word 'psychoanalysis' ought strictly to be confined to the particular method of psychotherapy employed by Freud and his followers. Since there are other equally effective methods, based on the work of Jung, of Horney, of Alexander and French, and many others, the term analytical psychotherapy or analysis will be used to denote the type of treatment which is to be discussed in this chapter. It may be taken to include any form of psychotherapy which consists of frequent, regular interviews over a period of months or years in which the therapist, without being didactic or authoritarian, attempts to help the patient to reach a better understanding of himself and his problems, and in which the relationship which develops between patient and analyst is itself discussed. Some analysts make use of dream analysis, some rely principally on free association; for others the reconstruction of early childhood is the core of the treatment, and for others still, the analysis of the transference situation is all important. All, however, have in common the general principle that their therapeutic task is to help the patient to help himself rather than to order his life for him: and they thus eschew hypnosis and other methods which depend upon the therapist's prestige rather than upon increasing the patient's capacity to direct his own affairs.

Analytical psychotherapy is not a standardized method of treatment which can be applied to a patient's mind as a plaster might be applied to his broken leg. It is an art, rather than a science; and its effects, which are often striking, depend upon a complicated and largely incalculable interaction between the personalities of the therapist and the patient. The effect of a new drug upon the body is often difficult to assess, because of the number of variables involved. It is still harder to measure the effect of psychotherapy upon the mind; and, at present, reliable statistics are rarely available. This is partly because psychotherapists have been unnecessarily reluctant to submit their results to critical scrutiny; and partly because these results are of a kind which, although they are important to the patient, cannot easily be classified statistically. For example, the disappearance of a particular symptom is not necessarily a reliable yardstick: for the relief of a patient's distress, which is the main task of the psychotherapist, may consist more in producing a change of attitude towards a symptom than in getting rid of it, and such changes of attitude are not accurately mensurable. A fetishist, for instance, may gain from psychotherapy alleviation of his guilt, increased self-confidence, and a much greater capacity for making a love relationship, and yet retain a certain interest in his fetish, or actually make positive use of it on particular occasions. A statistician who took as his criterion for the success of psychotherapy the complete disappearance of the symptom which had led the patient to seek help might regard such a case as a failure; but he would then be excluding from his survey some of the most valuable results which psychotherapy can bring about.

Psychotherapists are by temperament inclined to oppose the efforts of their academic colleagues to assess scientifically subtle changes in personality and attitude which seem beyond the scope of measurement: but if they are to extend the benefits of psychotherapy to more people than are now able to receive them, they must be able to demonstrate its effectiveness to sceptics. Fortunately, a new generation of psychiatrists is emerging which is trained both in analytical psychotherapy and in the methods of science; and the figures which are so far available indicate that psychotherapists have nothing to fear from statistical inquiry. It used to be alleged, for example, that it was almost unknown for male homosexuals to change over to heterosexuality; and the Wolfenden Committee was unable to discover a single case in which such a change had occurred. Every experienced therapist will usually refrain from holding out much hope of a complete changeover in such cases, although there are many instances in which psychotherapy can be of help to homosexuals. But it appears that even psychotherapists have underestimated the effectiveness of treatment. For a carefully controlled American study of 106 male homosexuals who undertook psychoanalysis revealed the following facts: of seventy-nine who began treatment as exclusively homosexual, fourteen (nineteen per cent) became exclusively heterosexual; while of thirty who began treatment as bisexual, fifteen (fifty per cent) became exclusively heterosexual. This same study also demonstrated that the likelihood of change is related to the length of treatment. This latter observation is also important, since those who object to analysis as a method of treatment usually do so on the grounds of its long duration.

There are many varieties of analysis: and, even within the same school, it has been shown that analysts differ considerably in the methods they employ. In spite of this, there is sufficient common ground between the various schools of analysis, as opposed to didactic methods of psychotherapy, for certain generalizations to be made about the principles of analytical treatment.

In the early chapters of this book, it was asserted that the sexual deviations generally originated in early childhood, and that those who developed these disorders suffered from feelings of both sexual guilt and sexual inferiority to an exaggerated degree. The therapist's prime task, therefore, must be to relieve his patient of the burden of guilt and inferiority which has prevented his sexual instinct from finding expression in the only fully satisfactory way known to human beings – a heterosexual love-relationship. It is difficult enough for the so-called normal person to be entirely honest and open about his sexual behaviour; for, as explained in an earlier chapter, everyone of us carries into adult life some feelings of guilt about sex. It is doubly difficult for the sexually deviant to reveal themselves: for, not only do they suffer from the original childish sense of excessive sexual guilt and inferiority which has given rise to the deviation, but they also labour under an additional load of similar feelings which is secondary to the deviation itself, even if this has only been imagined rather than performed. A child reared in an authoritarian household in which any manifestation of infantile sexuality is immediately punished, may, as a result, come to have sadistic phantasies in adolescence. The experience of being a prey of such phantasies thus increases his sense of guilt and inferiority still further, so that a vicious circle is created from which there seems no escape. Guilt about such things is sometimes so severe that it may take months for the patient to reveal himself, even though intellectually he may appreciate that the analyst's attitude will not be one of condemnation.

A full admission of sexual proclivities and practice is in itself a great relief to many patients, who still often imagine that they are uniquely wicked, that no one else has ever entertained such desires, and that it is quite impossible that anyone who knew their inmost thoughts could possibly accept or love them. The discovery that deviant impulses are universal, and that another human being can tolerate such impulses is a valuable beginning to treatment.

It is also important to the patient that the analyst is able to give a reasonable explanation of the origin of his symptoms. To be compulsively attracted by a piece of jewellery, or by a child, or by the anus rather than by the vagina, is so strange even to those who are the prey of such compulsions, that to discover that these things can be explained in rational terms is reassuring. Nothing is so alarming to human beings as the inexplicable.

Moreover, the psychotherapist is in a position to point out to the patient that even the most bizarre deviation has some positive value concealed within it. Most patients who come for treatment of these disorders regard their deviant impulses as totally unacceptable – an attitude which actually precludes any possibility of change. For, so long as a desire which is part of oneself is regarded as completely alien, it is impossible to come to terms with it or to modify it. Paranoid people regard their desires and their hostilities as having been instilled into them from without by enemies. Whilst those who are obsessed with deviant phantasies do not go as far as this, they find it extremely difficult to see that these things are actually part of their own nature and to take full responsibility for them. This necessary step becomes more conceivable when they can understand that, whilst it is undesirable or impossible to act upon many deviant phantasies, yet the latter contain the seeds of potentialities which are valuable, though incompletely realized parts of their personalities. The sadist, for instance, is generally a man who in actual life is too compliant, although in phantasy he is intensely dominant. Neither his real life nor his phantasy is satisfactory; but, were he able to unite the two, he might become a normally assertive individual. It is true to say that, to attain maturity, he needs something which is to be found in his phantasy even though this may at first appear totally unacceptable. An important part of the psychotherapy of sexual deviations consists, therefore, in demonstrating the positive value to be found in the deviant impulse so that the patient can learn to accept it and come to terms with it.

In most cases, however, confession and the establishment of intellectual insight are not enough to alter a deviant sexual pattern which has been established from early childhood. These patterns cannot simply be regarded as conditioned reflexes, but represent partial or complete failures in human relationships. They are essentially substitutes for loving a person, or at least for loving an adult person of the opposite sex. The fetishist has substituted his fetish for a woman, the paedophilic a child; the sadist can only dominate his partner, while the masochist can only yield. In homosexual relations it is true that a nearer approach is made to adult loving, and this may be one reason why the homosexual pattern is more difficult to alter than that of other deviations; but even the most stable homosexual relationship still falls short of the completeness which is found in heterosexuality.

The capacity to love another human being depends in the first instance, upon having oneself been loved; and it is those who, in childhood, have not been secure in the belief that they were totally accepted who, when they grow up, are incapable of either loving or believing that anyone could really love them in return. It is a remarkable and interesting aspect of human nature that a person's attitude to himself and his attitude to others is essentially the same. Those who hate and despise themselves are those who hate and despise other people; and, in order to be capable of loving another person, one must ultimately be capable of accepting oneself as one is and even of regarding oneself with a certain measure of approval.

Self-love is conventionally believed to be conceit; but the person who has none of it, and who genuinely hates his own nature, is incapable of love, and either makes impossible demands upon others for affection, or else withdraws himself as far as possible from human contact. In order to be able to give, a man needs the conviction that he has something within himself which is worth bestowing; and this degree of self-love is not arrogance, but a proper recognition that one is oneself a human being, no better possibly, but probably no worse than the rest of our dubious species.

A patient suffering from a sexual deviation will be able to exchange it for something better only if his capacity for adult love is actually enhanced. This can certainly come about; but it will happen only if circumstances enable him to make a new and better relationship with another person of such a kind that he is able to gain from it an inner conviction of being of some value. It is well known that sexually deviant phantasies and compulsions can disappear overnight if the man who is obsessed by them falls in love. But to be able to fall in love with a real person argues a degree of maturity which the deviant has not reached; and it is only when he is on the point of outgrowing his deviant tendency that he can relate himself emotionally to another person with sufficient confidence to fall in love. The most important part of the psychotherapist's task, therefore, is to provide the kind of background of complete acceptance and of emotional security against which the patient can mature, and from which he can finally depart to make other and more fruitful relationships elsewhere.

It may be supposed that to do this is an easy task, and that all that is required from the psychotherapist is a modicum of tolerance and compassion. In reality, however, this is the most difficult as well as the most rewarding aspect of the psychotherapeutic endeavour. A sexually deviant person, is, according to our present view, suffering from the effects of an early failure in the relationship between himself and his parents of such a nature that he did not feel himself loved as a whole, and thus came to regard himself as both inferior and bad. He may not easily be able to believe that any person, however compassionate or tolerant, will be able to accept him, since he cannot accept himself; and he will tend to regard the therapist as a judge who is likely to condemn him, rather than as someone who might be concerned to help him – just as he regarded his parents and other authorities in the past.

One of the reasons why analytical psychotherapy takes so long is that emotional attitudes which date from early childhood are slow to change; and it is only gradually that the patient can come to realize that he has been living in a hostile world, isolated by fear and guilt from being able to give and receive love freely. The great advantage of the psychotherapeutic situation over most other types of exchange between two human beings is that the psychotherapist is prepared, and indeed expects, to discuss and modify the relationship between the patient and himself. The technical term for this is the analysis of the transference situation; and it is undoubtedly the most potent factor in healing the patient.

When any of us confront an unknown person, especially a person in authority, we automatically attribute to him various qualities derived partly from our experience in similar situations in the past. In the chapter on female homosexuality, we discussed the psychological mechanism of projection, and gave as an example the way in which a girl may project upon an older woman an idealized feminine image. This is one way in which a real person may be distorted by a subjective preconception. In a psychotherapeutic situation, the patient generally projects many such figures upon the therapist, who himself deliberately remains partially unknown in order that he may be better able to study these figures. Any person asking for help is, for the moment, in something like the position of child to parent, *vis-à-vis* the person from whom he is seeking aid. It is therefore quite natural that a patient should project upon the therapist figures derived from childhood, especially those of his parents. He will, therefore, tend to behave as if the therapist were a parent who would both condemn him and make him feel inferior; even though he may realize intellectually that this is not the case.

Everyone has had the experience of correcting a wrong judgement about another person. As we get to know someone, we discover that they are cleverer or less intelligent, kinder or crueller, more interesting or less interesting than we had thought at first. This process of getting to know a person is partly one of withdrawing projections, of correcting misconceptions which we had made automatically about someone unknown to us.

In the relationship between therapist and patient, this process of withdrawing projections is of particular value; for by means of it, the patient is able to make that new and better kind of relationship with another person which we suggested was necessary if he was to be able to find some value in himself and a greater capacity to love his neighbour.

Ideally, therefore, the psychotherapy of the sexual deviations, in addition to giving the patient the opportunity of admitting his difficulties freely and of gaining an understanding of their origin, should be sufficiently prolonged to include the analysis of the transference situation. Once a man has had the experience of finding that there is at least one person who is prepared to accept and value him, he may be able to approach other people with an open mind, instead of feeling that he will be invariably rejected;

and in this way he may be able to achieve that deeply intimate relationship with another person in which normal love can flourish and in which deviant impulses lose their importance.

For, as we have so often reiterated, a sexual deviation is the outward and visible sign of a failure to make an adult love-relationship; and the study of sexual deviation is the study of sex without love. We have much to learn about the way human beings develop, and no doubt in time our methods of treatment will be superseded. No psychotherapist ought to rest content with a treatment which is so prolonged and expensive that it cannot possibly be offered in its present form to all those who would benefit from it. It is only very recently that Western man has begun to study his sexual life objectively, and our ignorance of this fundamental aspect of ourselves is still profound. Ignorance, prejudice, and condemnation invariably march hand-in-hand; and the sexually deviant are still too often regarded with the fear and horror which spring from lack of understanding. If this book, written for the general public, has demonstrated that sexually deviant people share the same human condition with us all, it will have succeeded in its purpose.

Bibliography

ALLEN, CLIFFORD, *The Sexual Perversions and Abnormalities*, London (O.U.P.), 1951.

BIEBER, IRVING, *et al.*, *Homosexuality, A Psychoanalytic Study*, New York (Basic Books), 1962.

BRITISH MEDICAL ASSOCIATION, *The Criminal Law and Sexual Offenders* (A report of the Joint Committee on Psychiatry and the Law appointed by the British Medical Association and the Magistrates' Association), London (B.M.A.), 1949.

CLEUGH, JAMES, *The Marquis and the Chevalier*, London (Andrew Melrose), 1951.

ELLIS, ALBERT, and ABARBANEL, ALBERT (Editors), *The Encyclopaedia of Sexual Behaviour*, London (W. Heinemann Medical Books), 1961 (2 vols.).

ELLIS, ALBERT, and BRANCALE, RALPH, *The Psychology of Sex Offenders*, Illinois (C. C. Thomas), 1956.

FENICHEL, OTTO, *The Psychoanalytic Theory of Neurosis*, New York (W. W. Norton), 1945.

FLUGEL, J. C., *The Psychology of Clothes*, London (Hogarth Press and Institute of Psychoanalysis), 1940.

FREUD, SIGMUND, *Collected Papers*, Vol. V, London (Hogarth Press and Institute of Psychoanalysis), 1950.
Three Essays on the Theory of Sexuality, London (Imago), 1949.

GLOVER, EDWARD, *The Social and Legal Aspects of Sexual Abnormality*, London (Institute for the Scientific Treatment of Delinquency), 1947

GUTTMACHER, MANFRED S., *Sex Offences*, New York (W. W. Norton), 1951.

HADFIELD, J. A., *Psychology and Mental Health*, London (Allen & Unwin), 1950.

HERON, ALASTAIR (Editor), *Towards a Quaker View of Sex*, London (Friends' Home Service Committee), 1963.

KINSEY, ALFRED C., *et al.*, *Sexual Behaviour in the Human Male*, Philadelphia (W. B. Saunders), 1948.
Sexual Behaviour in the Human Female, Philadelphia (W. B. Saunders), 1953.

LELY, GILBERT (trans. Alec Brown), *The Marquis de Sade*, London (Elek Books), 1961.

MEAD, MARGARET, *Male and Female*, London (Gollancz), 1950; Harmondsworth (Penguin Books), 1962.

RADZINOWICZ, L. (Preface), *Sexual Offences* (A report of the Cambridge Department of Criminal Science), London (Macmillan), 1957.

TAYLOR, G. RATTRAY, *Sex in History*, London (Thames & Hudson), 1953.

WEST, D. J., *Homosexuality*, Harmondsworth (Penguin Books), 1960.

Index

*Two other books published by Penguins
are described on the following pages*

STUDIES IN SOCIAL PATHOLOGY

There must be very few families which have not at some time or another been faced with an acute human crisis caused by a failed marriage, a suicide attempt, mental illness, alcoholic irresponsibility, sexual assault, or some other form of social and personal breakdown. Many forms of social illness are baffling and even frightening and an attempt to explain the pathology of social illness is now overdue.

STUDIES IN SOCIAL PATHOLOGY is under the general editorship of Professor G. M. Carstairs, Professor of Psychological Medicine at the University of Edinburgh.

Further titles to be published soon include

SUICIDE AND ATTEMPTED SUICIDE
Erwin Stengel

ALCOHOLISM
Neil Kessell

Future titles on marital disharmony, severe mental illness, and other forms of social and personal illness are planned.

Another Pelican Book by Anthony Storr

THE INTEGRITY OF THE PERSONALITY

'Self-realization is not an anti-social principle; it is firmly based on the fact that men need each other in order to be themselves.'

With this axiom of psychology Anthony Storr, at the outset of an excellent and simple study of human personality, counters the fear expressed by Bertrand Russell and others that analytical psycho-therapy may tend to produce an anarchical race of Byrons or Hitlers.

Tolerant and impartial in tone, his book stands securely on the ground that is common to Freudian, Jungian, and other schools of psychology. Maintaining that many roads lead to self-realization, he discusses in successive chapters the mental mazes of identification, introjection, projection, and dissociation, through which the individual, sooner or later, must find his way on the path to maturity.

'The book is well written, concise and clear, and is cordially recommended' – *Mental Health*

'He deals frankly, in comprehensible terms, with the hypotheses the therapist uses in treatment' – *British Medical Journal*

'His emphasis on the beliefs shared rather than the areas of controversy is right for a book intended for the lay public' – *Lancet*

For a complete list of books available please write to Penguin Books whose address can be found on the back of the title page